REFLECTIONS OF THE LOVE OF GOD

Jerry Glenn Kneeland

NEW HARBOR PRESS
RAPID CITY, SD

Copyright © 2021 by Jerry Glenn Kneeland.

All rights reserved. No part of this publication may be reproduced, distributed or transmitted in any form or by any means, including photocopying, recording, or other electronic or mechanical methods, without the prior written permission of the publisher, except in the case of brief quotations embodied in critical reviews and certain other noncommercial uses permitted by copyright law. For permission requests, write to the publisher, addressed "Attention: Permissions Coordinator," at the address below.

Kneeland/New HarborPress
1601 Mt. Rushmore Rd, Ste 3288
Rapid City, SD 57701
www.newharborpress.com

Ordering Information:
Quantity sales. Special discounts are available on quantity purchases by corporations, associations, and others. For details, contact the "Special Sales Department" at the address above.

Reflections of the Love of God/Jerry Glenn Kneeland. -- 1st ed.
ISBN 978-1-63357-241-6

Contents

Introduction 1

Getting to Know Kevin 5

Kevin Sees an Angel 7

Kevin's Baptism 11

Kevin goes to college. He quits college and then he has
several jobs and surgeries. 13

Kevin goes back to college and after graduating he goes
to graduate school. 17

Kevin's VISTA Training Experiences 21

Kevin's Thoughts during His Year in VISTA 27

Kevin decides to marry the woman he loves and to not
be a priest. 33

Kevin and his wife are rebaptized. 37

Kevin goes to the Episcopal church and is confirmed
in the Episcopal church 41

Kevin Attends a Cursillo 47

Kevin sees a supernatural light that turns into a golden
ball that continues to rise from the floor of his bathroom
and then breaks apart, filling his bathroom with golden light 53

Kevin is transported back into the past and he sees the Crucifixion of Christ and a vision of a shining steel cross without Christ on it, signifying that Jesus Christ has been resurrected.	59
Kevin sees the vision the Sacred Heart of Jesus.	67
Kevin is saved by a little mongrel brown dog that fought off a big black dog that wanted to attack Kevin.	73
Kevin struggles with his faith in finding a job and, not finding a job, he goes to graduate school.	77
While thinking about that sister that Kevin loved long ago, he starts thinking about his past.	87
Kevin's Life before Retirement	93
Kevin's Life after His Wife Died	101
God's Last Comments to Jason	107
Index of Visions and Supernatural Manifestations	115
Author's Note	117
About the Author	121

Introduction

JASON HAD JUST FINISHED graduating from high school. In school, he was a quarterback that had helped his team to place second in the state championship. Jason seemed to have all what it takes: he was popular in school, he had dated several girls, and there were girls that wanted to date him. Jason was not only good at football, he made very good grades in school. His parents were proud of him. His father was a professor at the local college, which was a leading school in the nation. His father had inherited a lot of money and property after his father had died. His mother did not have a profession, but she did help at several fundraisers for the local hospital.

Jason did not know what to do with his life. He might have been a very good football player and scholar in school. He knew he would miss all the popularity that he had at school. He was satisfied with his life at school; but, since he has graduated from school, he did not know what to now do with his life. There was something missing in Jason's life. He and his parents never went to church. He heard very little about Jesus. It never occurred to him to pray to God and ask him for guidance. It seemed to him that he could succeed at anything that he would apply himself to do. He told himself that he did not pray to a God that he did not know. He always had his parents, who gave him anything he wanted. He had a car, a TV, a stereo, a computer, and a smart phone.

That night after his graduation, he had a party with some of his friends to celebrate the occasion. After the party, he went home and told his parents good night and went to bed. He tossed and turned and had a hard time going to sleep. But finally he did fall asleep.

GOD

Jason, Jason. I want you to pay attention. Yes, you are asleep. But I want to help you. You need to have some plans about what kind of vocation you want to spend a lot of time working every week for most of your life. Also, life is more than just working, or making a lot of money. There has to be meaning in your life. You should get to know me. Who am I? I am your God. I hope that after you wake up from your dream, that you will know a little more about me. You see in life, you can be a success in your career—even in your marriage—but you can be spiritually dead. You can make a lot of money. You can buy luxury cars, expensive clothes, all kinds of electronic gadgets, but these possessions will not bring you happiness. You can have the most beautiful wife and make love to a beautiful woman, which to many men would be complete joy. But, Jason, without a sense of being close to Myself, to your God, the older you get, the less enjoyment that you will have from money, possessions, sex, and even love on the physical plane. Yes, you can love your wife if you love her heart and soul, besides her body. I am going to show you a life of a man that is named Kevin. In your dream, you are an observer. Kevin will not see or hear you, and you will not be able to talk with anybody, except with Me. I will now and then speak to you about some of Kevin's moments of living. I need to do this because there are times when Kevin's life seems horrible. But Kevin was helped by Me to guide his life and help him with the struggles of life. Yes, Jason, so far in your life everything seemed great. You were a champion football player, you had many dates with girls, you are very intelligent, and you made good grades in school. Your parents would give you many things. But you are young. You do not know what could be in store for your life. I hope when you observe Kevin's life, that it will help you in your life when you wake up.

• CHAPTER 1 •

Getting to Know Kevin

GOD

JASON, BEFORE I SHOW you some of the events in Kevin's life, I want to tell you something about Kevin. Kevin is what is called a "war baby." He was born in 1942, a time in which there was World War II. His father was a steelworker when he was born. His father and mother did not want to raise Kevin in a big city. So, his father went to work for a railroad. He was a freight agent and telegrapher. For a long time, Kevin's father was bumped from his job. Someone with more seniority can bump Kevin's father and take his job. And Kevin's father could also bump someone with less seniority than he had and take his job.

Kevin's father was drafted in 1944 when Kevin was two years old. Except for a trip that Kevin's mother took, in which she took Kevin to visit Kevin's father when he just finished his basic training, Kevin and his mother did not see Kevin's father and his mother's husband until his two years of service was completed. After Kevin's father completed his term of service, Kevin's father went back to work for the railroad. And so about every six months, Kevin and his parents had to move wherever Kevin's father has his new job. After Kevin started attending school, this became hard for Kevin. Every six months or so, Kevin had to attend a new school in a new town. It was hard for Kevin to make new friends at school. It seemed for Kevin that in every new school the kids all wore different clothes than what Kevin wore in his previous school. In one school, the kids all wore blue jeans while he wore dress pants. In another school, after Kevin made the adjustment of wearing clothes like the other kids, he again was dressed differently from them. So, in almost every new school in a new town, some of those kids would make fun of him. Kevin wore eyeglasses and so the kids called him "four eyes" or "professor." Kevin was even taught how to read two different ways.

I will tell you more about Kevin when I show you more moments and events from Kevin's life.

· CHAPTER 2 ·

Kevin Sees an Angel

GOD

JASON, IT IS TIME to begin your journey observing Kevin's life. I will show you different highlights of his life. I have already told you that you are an observer. No one will be able to see or hear you; but you will not only see and hear Kevin and other people, you will, in your mind, know even what Kevin is thinking.

Kevin is a ten-year-old boy. He goes to Sunday school in a Presbyterian church. The church is right across the street where Kevin lives. He lives in a small town and the church is near his home—so he walks to the church all by himself.

KEVIN IS IN HIS SUNDAY SCHOOL CLASS

The Sunday school teacher is a young woman that helps the church in any way she can. She says, "Christians are very happy when they follow Christ." Kevin then thinks about what his teacher has just said.

KEVIN'S THOUGHTS

I wonder why my parents don't seem happy all the time. I know they worry about being able to pay their bills. I believe they are Christians because they send me to Sunday school. But they don't go to church. Maybe if they go to church, they will be happier. I wonder if my teacher is telling the truth—for when I go to some of my friends' homes, the kids' parents don't seem to be happy. And when my parents are not happy, then I am not happy.

KEVIN IS SITTING ON HIS PORCH

He has been sitting now and then on that porch for most of the summer.

KEVIN'S THOUGHTS

I want to know if my Sunday school teacher is right. If she is right, all of us should be happier than we have been. I would like to talk to God, but I am just a kid. And I am not good enough to talk to God. But I would like to see an angel; an angel might be able to talk to me. I have been sitting on this porch almost every day. I have been hoping to see an angel. I do pray to God. I know he will not talk to me, but I hope he will let me see one of his angels.

Suddenly Kevin sees an angel. It was flying out of the steeple of the church that is right across the street. The angel was flying very fast.

KEVIN'S THOUGHTS

The angel is very beautiful. Its clothes are bright white and shining. Its wings are pinkish orange. I have never seen anything so beautiful. I have to tell Mom and have her come here. I want her to see that angel.

KEVIN

Mom, hurry. Let's go to the front porch. I have seen an angel. I want you to see that angel.

Kevin points to the angel. It is very high in the sky. It is moving very fast.

KEVIN

Look mom, there it is!

But Kevin's mom does not see the angel. And the angel is finally so high, that not even Kevin can see the angel.

KEVIN'S MOM

Kevin, I never saw your angel. The angel might have been the angel of death. One of the church's members had died. They had his funeral this morning. Kevin, do not tell anybody that you saw an angel. It will be a secret just between you and me.

GOD

Kevin, I want you to know that most people do not see angels. I know that you have prayed for most of the summer that you want to see an angel. Because you really wanted to see an angel, I let you see a brief glimpse of an angel. Your Sunday school teacher was partially right. If one is close to Me and tries to follow Me, that person will have an inner joy and love and peace. This is called *grace*. I give my grace to help people to follow Me and guide them through their life. Kevin, life and love are a mystery. One can never be completely happy in this world. Only in heaven can one be completely happy.

• CHAPTER 3 •

Kevin's Baptism

GOD

JASON, THE NEXT HIGHLIGHT of Kevin's life is his baptism. Kevin is now twelve years old. He and his parents and his sister moved again after his dad bumped someone and took his job as a railroad freight agent. In Kevin's neighborhood, there was a girl that he had made friends with. That girl lived two houses away from where he lived. That girl's father was a Sunday school teacher at a Baptist church. He invited Kevin to attend his Sunday school class, and Kevin did go to his classes.

Jason, you are now thinking why you should be shown Kevin's baptism. You had not gone to church or Sunday school. You had not been baptized because you didn't go to church or Sunday school, and your parents did not go to church. Jason, you do not know anything about baptism. Jason, you now see inside Kevin's church. You see the minister standing by a small concrete pool. Kevin enters the pool. The minister holds Kevin above the water. He puts a handkerchief on Kevin's mouth and nose. The minister then puts Kevin under the water and when he places Kevin in the water he states, "I baptize you in the name of the Father, the Son, and the Holy Ghost."

KEVIN'S THOUGHTS

Before I was baptized in a Baptist church, I had to be interviewed by my minister to see if I accepted Christ as my personal Lord and Savior. I had attended Sunday school for around two years while I was in the seventh and eighth grades in junior high school. In Sunday school most of our teachings were about the great men of the Bible. After the description of these great individuals of the Bible, a statement was made showing how those individuals showed Christ in themselves, even though Jesus Christ would not be born as the Baby Jesus many years later. Then, a teaching about Jesus Christ would be given by the Sunday school teacher. We would have Sunday school books with beautiful pictures about the teachings we were given. So, I knew Christ in my mind. I accepted Him in my mind. Then, when I was baptized, I accepted Christ in my heart. When I came out of the water, I felt fresh and good. It seemed that my body had electricity moving through it. I knew it was Christ.

• CHAPTER 4 •

Kevin goes to college. He quits college and then he has several jobs and surgeries.

GOD

JASON, IT IS HARD to show you Kevin in one of his classes and the several jobs that he had after he had quit college. It will be better that you hear the thoughts of Kevin when he was going to college and what jobs he had after college.

KEVIN'S THOUGHTS

I had to drop out of college. I just couldn't concentrate. I needed quietness in order to study. With the doors closed in my bedroom at my parents' house, I still could hear the television. And the straw that broke the camel's back was during my speech class. The students were to make remarks about what they liked and disliked as we walked across the stage. When I was walking, the professor said that I walked like a clown. All the students laughed. I could not take it anymore, so I quit college. My parents were really disappointed in me. And I am disappointed and depressed.

Later on, I finally found out why I was walking like a clown. I was developing ingrown toenails in both of my big toes. The big toes became infected. The doctor told me to soak my feet in Epsom salt. But it did not do me any good. For three years, off and on, I had to go to the hospital for an operation on my big toes. When I was able to walk with shoes and without crutches, I did become a railroad relief clerk for my dad. He was a railroad freight agent; he had several clerks working for him. When one of those clerks became sick or went on vacation, I took their place. I could have become a full-time clerk if I would move to Cicero, Illinois. But I didn't want to do this. I was afraid to be on my own. And then it was not too long that my other big toe needed another operation.

During the Christmas season, I sorted mail at the post office. I really didn't know what I wanted to do with my life. I wanted to go back to college. But I kept talking myself out of going back. I wondered if I could study and make passing grades. The only strange thing that gave me courage is a genealogy book, which my dad brought home from the lockbox at his bank. My mom and dad always told me that my dad's family married royalty, but that we did not have royal blood. But I read that book and found out that one of my great-great-great grandfathers had married a great-great-great granddaughter of King James V of Scotland—so, I did have royal blood. When I traced my ancestry back, I was a descendant of St. Louis IX of France, Eleanor of Aquitaine, William the Conqueror, and Charlemagne. So, I said to myself, if my ancestors could rule countries, then I could rule myself. So, I gained the confidence to go back to college. And when I changed doctors, I didn't have ingrown toenails anymore. I went back to college and graduated summa cum laude.

• CHAPTER 5 •

Kevin goes back to college and after graduating he goes to graduate school.

GOD

JASON, YOU HAVE JUST heard many of the thoughts of Kevin while he was going to Illinois College for the first time. You found out what happened to Kevin after he had quit college, his part-time jobs and the operations on his ingrown big toenails for a total of three years of operations. This was before he even went to college for the first time. Kevin did have many honors while going to college: he was on the dean's list and had a full tuition scholarship during the last three years of college; he was a member of his college's forensic team in which he got excellent awards in oratory and oral interpretation at other colleges participating in speech tournaments; and, he was a member of Who's Who in American Universities and Colleges; he graduated summa cum laude.

Then, Kevin goes to graduate school at a large university working for a master's degree in Theater Arts. He made good grades for the summer session at that university. However, it is a different story when he went to classes in the fall. He took an advanced acting class. Most of the students in class had already taken acting classes on the undergraduate level with the same professor that was teaching this graduate course. The professor talked about things they covered last year when they were undergraduates. Kevin was totally lost. He only took one acting class in college. He was taught how to be flower or a teapot or a tree. He was only acting in a part that he had chosen to act before the class. There was no actual teaching of acting. Now, Kevin was expected to know the academic theories of acting that he did not know anything about. Kevin knew that he was not going to pass that so-called acting class that still did not teach the students how to act. So, he quit graduate school before he flunked out. It was a shattering experience for an honor student at college to be forced to quit graduate school. He went home and stayed with his parents. Jason, I will now let you hear Kevin's thoughts during this time.

KEVIN'S THOUGHTS

After I quit graduate school, I was very depressed. It was embarrassing for me and my parents. I was an honor student in college. I believe that my parents were proud of me when I was going to college; they probably bragged about me to their relatives and friends. I felt like I had not only let myself down, but my parents were very embarrassed. But now I was home with my parents. I did not know what to do with myself. In the liberal arts college that I attended, I knew a little bit about academic subjects, but I had no vocational training for the outside world of work. Also, I felt that God was not helping me. In graduate school, my roommate was a Christian Scientist. He would spend hours studying the Christian Scientist manual *Science and Health*, written by Mary Baker Eddy. I wish I could be strong in my faith like my roommate. After I had quit graduate school, my roommate sent me that book that Mary Baker Eddy had written. And it did help me spiritually and even got me out of my depression.

But so far, for a job or career that I should choose, God did not help me. My parents were ashamed of me. What good did it do to make good grades in college, when in the outside world, I did not know what I wanted to do? I did not want to work on an entry-level job making only minimum wages. I could have done that without ever going to college.

I had to leave home. My parents barely spoke to me. I didn't want to go to another graduate school, especially because I didn't know what I wanted to be. I could not volunteer for the armed forces, since I had the handicap of dermographism. One day, when I was at the post office, I saw a brochure about VISTA—Volunteers in Service to America. It was a way for me to leave home. I did not have any bills; I was young and unmarried. It was a way that I could learn more about life, and I could help people. So, I applied to be a VISTA volunteer.

• CHAPTER 6 •

Kevin's VISTA Training Experiences

GOD

JASON, LET ME TELL you about Kevin's VISTA training experiences. Kevin joined VISTA. He was accepted, but he had to wait for six months before he was to start his training. That six-month waiting was hard. Kevin did try to prepare himself for this training. He was a little bit overweight, so he rode a bicycle exerciser. And he did lose weight. His parents did not understand what he was going to do. Most of the time, his parents hardly said a word to him. Finally, he received a ticket for a flight to a city one thousand miles away from his hometown. Kevin was feeling afraid. He knew he would not see his parents for a long time. But now he would not be around to embarrass them. All his parents could see was their son sitting and watching TV. Both parents worked and his sister was now married and in Hawaii where her husband was stationed in the air force. So, Kevin was alone most of the time. His father came home from work for lunch, but his father hardly said a word to Kevin.

But now Kevin was leaving for VISTA training in a city one thousand miles away. When he was home, he would see his parents at night after they got home from work. But in VISTA, he would be all alone.

When Kevin's flight arrived in that city of his destination, a shuttle bus took him to a hotel in which the only residents were the VISTA trainees and the VISTA trainers, except for the few workers that cooked and served the meals. He was shown to his room and was told that his roommate will not show up until the next day. Kevin was feeling lonely; he was homesick. All he could do was read, for there was no TV or radio in his room.

The next day all the VISTA trainees were to gather for breakfast. They were welcomed by their trainers. After breakfast, the trainees were told that there would be no activities for the day. So, all of the trainees went back to their rooms. The next day, the trainees met in a large room with large tables. They were given a training manual and was told something about what they were going to do. Some days, there would be classes before breakfast and that class would last until suppertime. Other days, class would not start until midday and it would last until eight in the evening. Some days, there would be no classes. All of this unusual training was to teach the trainees what the trainers called *ambiguity*—to prepare oneself to never expect what one thought should happen in training and in life.

The speakers at the training sessions were from all walks of life and from many different cultures and races. Some of the speakers were Indians and some were Spanish or Mexican Americans who called themselves *Chicanos*. Some speakers worked with young people and other speakers worked with the elderly.

One day, the trainees were told to hand over their billfolds and watches. All they could keep were their Social Security cards. They were told to go out into the city and see how many jobs they could get hired for. This would be quite an experience for the trainees: all had long hair and they all wore blue jeans and combat boots. Of course, with the way the trainees looked, it would be unlikely that any one of them would be hired. The trainees were to see how many jobs they would get, but not to actually work at those jobs. Kevin and some of his friends were given a job to unload a truck carrying coffee cans. They were told to report to work in the afternoon. Of course, Kevin and his friends did not show up to work.

KEVIN'S THOUGHTS

I and my friends did get one job. Many of the trainees did not find even one job. But this is what to be expected because of the way we were dressed. After our workday was completed, we trainees were told to sleep at a flophouse and to not come back to the hotel until the following morning. Well, no trainee slept at any flophouse. I told my friends that there was no way that I would sleep at a flophouse; I was going to the railroad passenger station and sit up all night. One of my friends said that he had a friend attending a university that is thirty miles away. He was staying in a dormitory and that we would have a place to sleep. We did not have a car and no way to purchase a ticket on a bus. So, we hitchhiked. After a while I was crippling. My friends asked me what was wrong. I told them that I had an allergy to skin pressure called *dermographism*. I did not tell VISTA about my condition because if they knew, I would not have been accepted. We did get a ride after we walked a few miles. I got the bed at the dormitory because I was crippling. The next morning we hitchhiked back to the hotel; this time we got a ride very quickly. When the trainers found out that not one trainee slept in a flophouse, they were disappointed. Us trainees were about thirty in what was known as the Colorado 30.

Another time, I was told to spend the night at an emergency room at one of the city's hospitals. I was just to observe. Another time, I was told to go to a fancy strip joint to just observe.

At another time in our training, we were told that for a week we were to stay at a house in a Black neighborhood. The guys would stay in one house; the girls would stay in another house. There was no running water; there was a well for water. There was no indoor bathroom; there was an outhouse. The only stove for heat was an old wood and coal stove. There were no beds; we were given paper sleeping bags. There was a community center not far from our houses. At that center was a day-care center for children, a meeting room for the Black Panthers, and a room for the senior citizens. We were to spend a day at each one of those organizations. We were fed at the center.

At another time of our training, we were to undergo what was called *La Familia*—in which we were to stay with a low-income family and to help with their chores. I learned how to chop wood. I also helped to dig an irrigation ditch.

As part of our training, we were taken to the mountains. We climbed one mountain until we were above the tree line. We were to gather firewood for a campfire. To get to the place where we would have a cookout was a place across the Rio Grande River. Us trainees were told to walk across that river; the river was low enough so that we could walk across it. I told the trainers that they were crazy and that there was no way that I would walk across that river. Well, one of the trainees was a lady in her sixties. She started walking across that river. So, I told myself that if that lady could walk that river, then I could walk that river, too. And I did walk across that river. I should say that the river was cold and the current was very fast. We had to walk slowly so that the current would not take us down the river—which was the part of the river that was mostly very deep.

It was a nice cookout. I had the biggest steak that I ever had eaten. After a while, we did some singing around that campfire. I did enjoy myself. But that night, we had to walk back across that river. Now, it was dark and there were no lights. The trainers had a large rope extended to help us walk across. The trainers did help us to cross that river.

Us VISTAs were staying at a hotel in Monte Vista, Colorado. But that night, I got sick. I was nauseated and had a headache. That night many of us trainees got very sick. Finally, we were taken to the local hospital. We spent the night there. The next morning, a doctor told us that we had caught a bug. Many of us trainees thought it was food poisoning.

On the way back to Denver, our main training place, we got to see the white sands of New Mexico. We were given a tour of the Air Force Academy in Colorado Springs, too. Even though, for the most part, I enjoyed my training, there were some trainees who couldn't take the training; they quit and went home.

For our graduation, where we were given certificates and we were given a banquet at the University of Colorado in Boulder. We were told that we now had the equivalent of eight graduate semester hours in social work. We were told that our employer was the President of the United States, and that we had the equivalent rank of a Lieutenant Colonel.

The next day, at the hotel in Denver, we were given our assignments, which could be anywhere in the United States. Our training lasted for eight and a half weeks. I had wanted to work with American Indians at an Indian reservation. That did not happen. I and my hotel roommate were given the same assignment. We were to go to a small town in Colorado. We were to work with senior citizens who were mostly Spanish and Mexican Americans—and many of them had a trace of Indian blood. However, their culture was American, with some Spanish and Mexican customs and food, though the food and music were only for certain ceremonies of the Catholic church. In their everyday way of life, these senior citizens were very American.

• CHAPTER 7 •

Kevin's Thoughts during His Year in VISTA

KEVIN'S THOUGHTS

I WAS ASSIGNED TO a small town in Colorado. My roommate that I had in VISTA training still became my roommate at our new assignment. We took a bus which would take us to that small town. It was wonderful to see the mountains in the distance as we were going to our destination. It was very beautiful, especially since there were no mountains in my hometown, which was one thousand miles away.

We finally arrived at that small town—which according to VISTA was the target area. The house that we stayed in was made of adobe. The street in front of our house was unpaved. Where we lived, a paved street was a block and a half from our house. The unpaved street was hard enough to walk on when it didn't rain. And it was good that our town was a *semidesert*, an area that don't get much rain. However, when it did rain, the unpaved road became very muddy and hard to walk on. As I walked to the senior citizen center down that unpaved street, it seemed that everyone on that block and a half had a dog, and it seemed that all those dogs were barking at me as I tried to get to that paved street.

The senior citizen center was in an abandoned store that was situated along the only highway that went down the small town. At first, there were no visitors or clients that came to the center. I had to call the senior citizens to invite them to come to the center. It took several months before we had any clients that did come to the center. At the center, we had a knitting session in which the senior citizens continued working on what knitting they were already doing in their homes.

Then, the senior citizen center moved to an abandoned movie theater. The building was divided into two parts: the front part was a restaurant and the back part of the building was a large room that had a few tables and chairs. In the back, we had a desk and a phone. At this center, we didn't have any scheduled events since our stay was only temporary. Then, again we moved to our new senior citizen center which was a nice big house owned by the Presbyterian church that was next door. That church gave us the use of that building for the senior citizen center.

Most of the time, I was alone at the center, except for that knitting session that met once a week. One of the Catholic priests would drop by the center almost every day. I would make a large pot of coffee and we drank coffee and talked with each other. I became a close friend to that priest before I knew anything about the Catholic church.

Most of my senior citizens were Spanish and Mexican Americans. I knew that most of them went to the Roman Catholic church. So, I started attending the Catholic church to try to understand the culture of my senior citizens. I only went to observe. Before I ever went to the Catholic church, I asked myself how can anyone believe that bread and wine can change into the Body and Blood of Christ. However, the very first time that I went to Mass, I saw that the Holy Communion was real at the moment of consecration. And the people were so still that it was very quiet. Everyone was very serious as they received the Holy Communion. I knew something real was happening. I knew that there was something special about it. Of course, I did not receive Holy Communion, for I was only an observer.

Since I was a VISTA Volunteer, the Catholic sisters asked me if I could help them. They wanted me to help set up chairs at home Masses and to drive them in their car to conferences. I said that I would help. When I took the sisters to conferences, the people thought I was a priest; they even called me "Father." After the conferences the sisters would attend Mass before going home. There were two sisters and I sat between them. Those sisters taught me about the Holy Communion. I still did not go forward to receive it, but I began to feel the Holy Spirit, even before I started to receive Holy Communion. I began to feel the Holy Communion not only at Mass, but all the time outside of Mass. One of the sisters gave me some books to read about the Catholic church, and that Sister called me her "Son."

At one of the home Masses, the priest (a different priest that came to the center to talk with me) asked me if I would like to receive Holy Communion. And I did receive, and I felt the Holy Spirit. And from that moment on, when I had my First Communion, I always received Holy Communion. It is hard to describe how I feel when I attend Mass and receive Holy Communion, but I feel fresh and good and peaceful and joyful.

I wanted to do something to find a way for my senior citizens to feel that they belonged to their community and that all people of all cultures should feel equal to each other. So, I produced and directed a variety show. I had several bands that came to the senior citizen center to practice in the evening. Two Catholic sisters came and sang a song together. My senior citizens in the daytime sang several songs that I had selected for them. All songs were in English, except the French song "Farajaka." The variety show was a success. We used the abandoned theater that was once our senior citizen center.

For Christmas, I produced and directed a play about the Nativity. My senior citizens' grandchildren were my actors and actresses. My senior citizens made the costumes for the play. Some of my senior citizens' children helped build the set for the play. The play was performed for the community, and it was very successful.

I wanted to do something to help the Catholic church. So, I thought we would have a religious pageant or procession in honor of St. Benedict and St. Scholastica. In life, these two saints were actually brother and sister to each other. I designed one banner to honor St. Benedict and one banner to honor St. Scholastica. I read several articles about these two saints and what each one was known for. I put a symbol or a phrase on each banner to represent each saint. I then picked quotations from the Bible and had each senior citizen pick one of these verses. The seniors were then to go home and make their chosen banners that they would carry in the procession. I chose a song, "Las Mañanitas," that was in Spanish, but the two sisters and myself, who did not know how to speak Spanish, used a Spanish–English dictionary to translate. I wrote an article in the local newspaper about the pageant and invited the community to see us proceed down the main street of the town. Our parish priest led our pageant and carried a banner that I designed. One of my senior citizens made that banner. We proceeded down main street singing "Las Mañanitas" in both Spanish and English. I also wrote a paper about the two saints of our procession, and gave a copy to everyone at the center. Father asked me if I would give a sermon in the church once a month. Even though I was seriously thinking about becoming a priest, I told him no because I did not know enough about the Catholic church.

There was one place that I still felt lonely—that was at home. I had a roommate, but he was gone most of the time. He worked at a senior citizen center in a town that was ten miles away from the center that I worked at. In the morning, I would leave early and my roommate was still sleeping or he had not come home. And, at times, when he did come home, I was already in bed. So, at home I felt lonely quite a lot of the time.

One time, I was trying to go to sleep. I was feeling very lonely. Before I had a chance to lay down, I knew that my grandmother was in my bedroom. I do not known why I knew it was my grandmother, my dad's mother, for she died when I was around three years old. My mother had told me that my grandmother really liked me—that she called me her "Little Man." But, for some reason, I knew my grandmother was there. It was a feeling that there was sort of peace and love and joy all together. I even felt for a moment that I was not even in my bedroom. Then, I felt that she was telling me goodbye. And then she was no longer in my bedroom. But I felt different. I no longer felt lonely. I felt good and fresh and even exhilarating.

• CHAPTER 8 •

Kevin decides to marry the woman he loves and to not be a priest.

KEVIN'S THOUGHTS

EVEN THOUGH I TURNED down that opportunity to preach once a month at the Catholic church, I still felt that God was calling me to be a priest. However, it does seem strange that being a strong Baptist in my childhood and adolescence that I would even decide to be a priest. I know what some of the Protestants believe. Some of them think that Catholics are not saved—that they have not accepted Jesus Christ as their personal Lord and Savior. And that was what I believed when I attended the Baptist church. But there are different ways to look at something. As a Baptist, I first believed in Christ when I was going to Sunday school. I know what the Baptist church and the Bible beliefs are according to the Baptists. Jesus told Nicodemus that he had to be born again—to follow Christ in your mind and heart and so that person would then be saved. But, in the Catholic church, a person as a child learns what is Holy Communion and that if a person partakes and receives the Body and Blood of Jesus Christ, then Christ is with that person. This is another way of saying that when a person, usually at ten years of age, makes his or her First Communion, that person accepts Christ in his or her mind and heart; and so, as the Catholic child accepts Jesus Christ in both mind and heart, the Catholic child is born again and has accepted Jesus Christ as his or her personal Lord and Savior.

As a priest, I would be able to bless the bread and wine with the Holy Spirit changing the essence of the bread and wine into the Body and Blood of Christ. This was one of the reasons why I felt that I was being called to be a priest. The Holy Communion is receiving Christ when one eats the bread and drinks the wine. The outward appearance of the bread and wine still seem to be bread and wine, but the inner essence of the bread and wine has been changed into Christ within their elements. It would have been an honor to bless the bread and wine and, with the Holy Spirit, change the essence of the bread and wine into the Body and Blood of Christ. I was calling myself a Catholic for I believed in the Mass and the Holy Communion. When I say the Lord's Prayer, I feel the presence of Christ before I even receive the Holy Communion. I even feel the Holy Spirit all the time; but during the Mass, I feel the Holy Spirit more. And so I felt that I was being called to be a priest.

I fell in love with one of the daughters of my senior citizens. I still thought about being a priest, but I could not live my life without the girl that I fell in love with. I even believed that if God wanted me to become a priest, He would allow married men to become priests. But this did not happen. Of course, I did not expect God to change the Catholic church for my aspirations.

Even though I was happily married, I still felt that I was being called to be a priest. But I did not feel that I was letting God down by being married. According to the Catholic church, marriage is a sacrament. When I got married, I intensely felt the Holy Spirit. God blessed me and my wife. We each become Christ for each other. When we loved each other, we were loving God.

I should share my thoughts about the priesthood of the Catholic church. It should not make a difference whether a man is married or not; if the man has been consecrated as a priest, that man should be able to bless the bread and wine in the Mass. It does seem strange that the Eastern part of the Catholic church allows a married man to become a priest. It should not matter where the man lives—East or West—for God is everywhere and the Mass is said all over the world. And an Episcopal priest can decide to be a Catholic priest. He has to go to a Catholic seminary for one year and be ordained again. Then, the Episcopal priest would then be a Catholic priest—and he can still be married and have his family. What should happen is that a married priest will still take a vow of chastity and obedience. If the married man is true to his wife, he is chaste. The Catholic church can still allow a single man to become a priest but, at the same time, a married man should be allowed to be a priest. If an Eastern Catholic and an Episcopal Catholic should be allowed to be a priest, then a married Western Catholic should be allowed to be a priest, too.

• CHAPTER 9 •

Kevin and his wife are rebaptized.

GOD

JASON, YOU SHOULD KNOW more about Kevin's wife. When Kevin married his wife, he did not know that she had mental problems. And these mental problems became worse as time passed. She developed clinical depression and Kevin was told that she had overlays of schizophrenia, too. Kevin's wife did see a psychiatrist that did not prescribe medications, and so her condition did not improve. She then saw another psychiatrist that did prescribe medications and her condition improved. But she still was not cured; she had days in which she was still depressed—but the depression was not as severe as it was in the past. Kevin thought that since his wife was a cradle Catholic that it would help her to go to confession. Jason, it is time for you to hear the thoughts of Kevin.

KEVIN'S THOUGHTS

I took my wife to see a priest that was a pastor of a church that was twenty miles away from where I and my wife lived. My wife did not want to see her local priest. It is true that a priest cannot divulge any thoughts or feelings that the penitent has discussed and confessed in the confession. But the town we lived in was a small town and even though my wife could still be secluded away from the priest, he probably would know who was doing the confession. And this can be an embarrassing position for the penitent. So, we did drive that twenty miles to see a priest that she did not know. After the confession, my wife did seem a little better; however, some of her days she still would be slightly depressed—which is a normal response for people who have clinical depression.

Still, I wanted to help my wife as much as I could. I took my wife to talk with a priest but not necessarily undergoing another confession—but to talk with a priest that she was close to when she was a teenager. The priest listened, and then he said that he wanted to rebaptize both of us—that the Holy Spirit would help us as we participated in the Sacrament of Baptism. The priest said that our first baptism was what counted. He dressed each one of us in a white robe. He put on his vestments. He gave us each a booklet that had Bible passages, the Apostles' Creed, and the renouncing of Satan and his ways of influencing the minds and souls of people. As we read the words in the booklet, we were confessing our faith in the Catholic church. Then, the priest poured water on our foreheads and, as he did this, he said: "I baptize you in the name of the Father, the Son, and the Holy Spirit." And to my surprise, I really felt the Holy Spirit.

Why was this a surprise to me? Yes, I have been going to Mass and receiving the Holy Communion. I have studied some of the doctrines and practices of the Catholic church. I was so filled with the Holy Spirit that I believed that God was calling me to be a priest. I did in a way give up being a priest because I fell in love with a beautiful woman. I did not want to lose that woman and the love that we shared with each other. And I believed that if God wanted me to be a priest, He would provide a way for me to be a priest and to be married. And when I was married, I really felt the Holy Spirit—even more than when I received Holy Communion, and even more than the feeling of the Holy Spirit when I was with VISTA thinking about being a priest. In VISTA, I was helping people. I did not care about how much money I was making. I felt good to be able to help people. So, in some ways, I felt like I was a priest. But, after my wedding and experiencing the Holy Spirit tremendously, I never experienced the Holy Spirit all the time. I only experienced the Holy Spirit in the Mass.

So, why was I surprised when I felt the Holy Spirit when I was baptized again? I guess because when I went to the Baptist church, I was taught that the only real baptism was when a person is immersed in deep water. So, I guess I still subconsciously felt that to be really baptized a person should be immersed in water. But this is not true. Even though the baptism was a rebaptism, I felt the Holy Spirit just as much as when I was baptized in the Baptist church. It does not matter how much water is used in the Sacrament of Baptism. And I should say that my wife's condition did improve. Of course, her condition could not be cured, but my wife felt the Holy Spirit and this has helped her cope with her condition. Now, she has really improved.

• CHAPTER 10 •

Kevin goes to the Episcopal church and is confirmed in the Episcopal church.

GOD

JASON, KEVIN NEVER GAVE up the idea that I was calling him to be a priest. He knew that since he was married in the Western part of the Catholic church, he could not be a priest. So, he wondered if there is a church that is very similar to the Catholic church. So, Kevin started reading about different churches; he discovered the Episcopal church. That church seemed just perfect for Kevin. The Episcopal church believes in all of the seven sacraments of the Catholic church. The minister is even called "Father." So, Kevin thought that he could start going to the Episcopal church and that, maybe, he could go to a seminary and become an Episcopal priest. When Kevin was going to the Episcopal church, he didn't know that the Catholic church would begin to allow an Episcopal priest to become a Catholic priest. Kevin thought that the Episcopal church was actually part of the Catholic church, so he was content to be an Episcopal priest. When the Anglican church decided that women could become priests, there were Anglican (and Episcopal) priests who did not believe that women should be allowed to do so. The Episcopal church is a part of the Anglican church but, in several countries, the Anglican church is called the Episcopal church. So, when this decision was made by the Anglican and Episcopal churches, Kevin thought that if he could be an Episcopal priest, he could find a way to be a Catholic priest. What would the Episcopal priest have to do to become a Catholic priest? He would have to attend a Catholic seminary for one year; he would have to be ordained again by the Catholic church. And when he becomes a Catholic priest, he could then keep his wife and family. It should be known that there are many Episcopalians and Anglicans who do not believe in the Pope and that the Pope is infallible. However, the High Church of the Episcopal and Anglican churches believes in the Pope.

So, Jason, Kevin started going to the Episcopal church; however, since he was going to a new and different church, Kevin did not receive Holy Communion until he was invited by the Episcopal priest to start receiving it. Kevin still went to the Catholic church on Saturday nights and to the Episcopal church on Sunday mornings. Eventually, Kevin was confirmed in the Episcopal church. Jason, now I want you to hear Kevin's thoughts.

KEVIN'S THOUGHTS

I thought that I could find a Protestant church that was similar to the Catholic church. This is hard because I believe in all the sacraments of the Catholic church. The Baptist church and the Disciples of Christ church do not believe in all the seven sacraments of the Catholic church. In those churches, they believe that the Lord's Supper, the Holy Communion, is symbolic; but the Communion calls to mind in the believer the Crucifixion of Christ and that, as one partakes of the Communion, one remembers that Christ died to forgive our sins. But the bread and grape juice are not changed into the Body and Blood of Christ. I read about the Episcopal church and found out that they believe in all the sacraments of the Catholic church, too. Even some of believers in the High Church of the Episcopal church believe that the Pope is the Vicar of Christ on Earth.

So, I went to the Catholic Mass on Saturday nights and the Episcopal Mass on Sunday mornings. I knew that the Catholic church believed that the Episcopal sacraments are not valid. However, I felt so strongly that God was calling me to be a priest, even though I was married, and that in the Episcopal church I could become an Episcopal priest. At first, I did not receive the Holy Communion in the Episcopal church; but, eventually, the Episcopal priest asked me if I would like to start receiving the Holy Communion. Of course, I said yes and from then on I received Holy Communion at every Episcopal Mass.

After a while, I told the Catholic pastor why I was going to both the Catholic church and the Episcopal church. He told me that if I did not become a priest, I would be frustrated for the rest of my life. He told me that I could receive the Holy Communion in the Episcopal church and that my wife could go to the Episcopal church and receive Holy Communion there. And so, I and my wife went to both the

Catholic church and the Episcopal church. In both churches, I and my wife felt the Holy Spirit.

After I went to the Episcopal church for quite some time, I was asked if I would like to be confirmed. I did say yes and started going to confirmation classes that was taught by the Episcopal priest.

When I was twelve years old, I was baptized in the Baptist church. I felt the Holy Spirit when I was baptized. When I was twelve, I did not know anything about confirmation—for in the Baptist church no one was ever confirmed. When I thought that God was calling me to be a priest, I studied the Catholic doctrines, beliefs, and practices. That was when I found out about confirmation. It is one of the seven sacraments of the Catholic church, and so are baptism and marriage. In my experience as a Baptist, I only experienced the Holy Spirit when I was baptized. I did not experience the Holy Spirit when I received Communion. The bread and wine are not transformed into the Body and Blood of Christ; however, when I did receive Communion when I partake of the bread and grape juice, I did call to mind the Crucifixion of Christ. By his death and resurrection, our sins can be forgiven and, as Christ rose from the dead, when we believe in Christ and His resurrection, we would be resurrected—that our soul is immortal and cannot die.

As I was being confirmed, the Bishop placed his hands on my head and said that I was being sealed by the Holy Spirit. This was like when the apostles Peter and John laid their hands on people who had been baptized, but had not received the Holy Spirit. As the Bishop laid his hands on my head, I felt the Holy Spirit more than I had ever experienced before. I feel fresh and good, like electricity is moving in my entire body. I feel joyful and powerful at the same time.

• CHAPTER 11 •

Kevin Attends a Cursillo

GOD

JASON, I WANT TO tell you about a movement in the Catholic and Episcopal churches. The movement was founded by Eduardo Bonnin in 1948. He was a Catholic layman who lived in Majorca, Spain. It was originally founded to train Christian leaders. It is now for any Catholic or Episcopalian to attend a three day and night retreat. During those three days, a group of men or women would gather together with no contact with the outside world—no newspapers, radio, television, and telephones. It is a course taught by priests and laymen that teaches about the Trinity and the essential truths of the Church and about being a friend to Christ. At this retreat, one is provided meals and there is time to make new friends. One is provided a cot for sleeping in at night.

At this time, Kevin and his wife were going to the Catholic Mass on Saturday nights and the Episcopal Mass on Sunday mornings. The Catholic pastor of Kevin's church told him that it was okay for him and his wife to go to the Episcopal church and receive the Holy Communion. This is unusual for a priest to allow a Catholic to receive

Holy Communion in any other church that is not Catholic. And this would be very unusual for the Catholic church has stated that the Episcopal sacraments are not valid. Also, the Catholic pastor had told Kevin that if he did not become a priest, he would be frustrated the rest of his life. And, Jason, I should say that Kevin was frustrated for the rest of his life because he did not become an Episcopal priest; and, of course, he couldn't be a Catholic priest because he was a married man in the Western part of the Catholic church.

Kevin heard about the Cursillo because he had a brother-in-law who had attended one. The men go to the Cursillo first and then their wives would attend a separate Cursillo from the men. Kevin did go to this retreat first, and then his wife went to her Cursillo.

The lessons taught at the Cursillo helped Kevin to know more about the Holy Spirit, more about Me, since I am God the Father, the Son, and the Holy Spirit. On the second day of this retreat, the men were to go to confession—or what it is now called *Reconciliation*. Kevin was the only man at this retreat who was not a cradle Catholic, for Kevin had a Protestant background in the Baptist and the Disciples of Christ churches, which are part of the denomination called the *Christian church*. In the churches that Kevin attended, as a Protestant, they didn't have the Sacrament of Reconciliation—or what is also known as *confession*. In his tradition, the people of these Protestant churches believed in praying to God—to Me, rather than having a priest to pray for the forgiveness of the sins committed by the penitents. These Protestants believed that when they prayed to Me, I would forgive their sins. And I should say that I would forgive their sins, and those sins would not be remembered. It was as if they had not sinned at all. What does the Bible say about the forgiven being as white as the driven snow? My Son, Jesus, said when He was on the Cross, "Father, forgive them, for they do not know what they are doing." And my Son meant that He was not only praying for the people who crucified Him, but for all the sinners of all the generations of the future.

In the Catholic church, they believed that a serious sin—called a *mortal sin*—would have to be forgiven in the confession to a priest—who would call on Me—the Holy Spirit—to forgive their sins. And I would forgive those sins for this Sacrament of Reconciliation or confession is truly a sacrament. However, the Catholics believe that all forgiven sins would still have to paid for. The priest, after he hears a confession and he believes that the sinner has remorse for having committed sin, gives penance to the sinner. *Penance* is actually another word for *punishment*. The Catholics believe that a person who had sinned must undergo some form of punishment or penance, which could be the sinner saying maybe ten Hail Mary or some other form of penance that fits the sin that was committed. The Catholics believe that if one has not completely paid for his sins while he was living, he completes paying for his sins in purgatory. I do not like that word *purgatory* implying that sins are purged in purgatory. Purgatory is a place for Christians who have accepted Me as their Savior, but have not completely loved Me. They were not close to Me. So, purgatory is a place of meditation and prayer. And it is beautiful. There is no punishment. And after the person gets close to Me and loves Me, then that person would go to heaven. Jason, there is a purgatory.

Jason, since all the men in this retreat went to the Catholic church and entered the confessional, he did not want to be the only person who didn't go to confession, so, he did. His confession was a little different from that of others. So, Jason, it is now time for you to hear Kevin's thoughts during his Cursillo.

KEVIN'S THOUGHTS

I enjoy the Cursillo. I am learning more about the Holy Spirit. But I do not want to know about the Holy Spirit; I want to feel the Holy Spirit. When I went to confession, I told the priest that I was from a Protestant background. I told him I have learned a lot about the Catholic church—that I have made my First Communion and I have been baptized by a Catholic priest—so, I call myself Catholic, even though I don't believe in everything that the Catholic church believes. However, I told the priest that I believe in all the seven sacraments of the Catholic church. I told him that I feel that God was calling me to be a priest—and even now that I am a married man. So, as a priest or as a Protestant, I would preach about Christ and the Trinity. If I would stay a Catholic, then I could not become a priest. If I would be a Protestant, I would be able to be a minister and to be allowed to preach. So, I told the priest that I didn't know if I should be a Catholic or an Episcopalian or a Baptist, the church I was baptized in when I was twelve years old. I told him that I was going to the Catholic Mass and the Episcopal Mass. The priest laid his hands on my head, and he said that God will help me—that He would show me what I should be.

On the third day, the last day of the Cursillo, we were told after dinner that we should go to our cots to pray and go to sleep early. We should have silence and to not talk with each other. I did pray to God for a while, but I could not go to sleep early and I could not spend hours praying to God. It would be good if I could pray to God for hours, but I couldn't do this. So, I sat on my cot and was in silence for several hours. Finally, I did go to sleep. The next morning we awoke hearing bells ringing. We were told to get out of bed. We entered a large room where we had gathered for meals in the parish center next to the church. The room was filled with people, both men and women, who had already made their Cursillos. They all had little bells and they were ringing them. Then, they hugged us and thanked us for making the Cursillo. I did feel the Holy Spirit. I remembered what Christ said in the Bible that when two or three people are gathered in His name, that He is in their midst. Well, Christ was there; God was there—God the Father, the Son, and the Holy Spirit.

• CHAPTER 12 •

Kevin sees a supernatural light that turns into a golden ball that continues to rise from the floor of his bathroom and then breaks apart, filling his bathroom with golden light.

GOD

JASON, EVEN THOUGH KEVIN was confirmed in the Episcopal church, he was still going to both the Episcopal Mass and the Catholic Mass. When Kevin was confirmed in the Episcopal church, he did experience My Presence, the Holy Spirit. But Kevin was experiencing My Presence in both the Episcopal and Catholic Masses. He did not know for sure that I was calling him to still be a priest. And if he would become a priest, he would have to be an Episcopal priest because he was married. In the Catholic church, there was a priest who told him that if he did not become a priest that he would be frustrated the rest of his life. That priest was a charismatic priest. He would play the guitar and sing beautifully and he preached from not only the church doctrines, but expressing himself from his heart. He expressed what he personally believed and about himself. Many people of that Catholic parish loved this priest; and Kevin did love that priest. It is true that many Catholic priests are very impersonal and just talk about church doctrine and the Bible, and never talk about themselves and their personal feelings. Kevin was feeling My Presence, the Holy Spirit, more in the Catholic church than in the Episcopal church. But if he decided to be completely a Catholic, he would never be a priest. So, Kevin was a little bit confused. He remembered what that priest had told him when he attended the Cursillo—that I would show him what he should be—whether he be Catholic, Episcopalian, or even Baptist.

One day, Kevin was so satisfied and pleased with the Catholic church and that charismatic priest in his local church. And so, if he'd decide to be Catholic, then he would give up his feeling that he was called to be a priest. However, the next day or so, Kevin still felt that he was still called to be a priest, so he would have to be Episcopalian.

Kevin would tell his wife his thoughts and his struggles; and his wife was a little bit tired of hearing Kevin's problems in choosing which church he would finally settle on and be satisfied. So, Kevin told his wife that if he could believe in the Immaculate Conception, then he would be Catholic. Kevin had a book about Mary and he was reading about the Immaculate Conception. At the same time that Kevin was reading, he saw a vision that would convince Kevin that he should be Catholic. So, Jason, it is now time for you to hear the thoughts of Kevin.

KEVIN'S THOUGHTS

I am arguing with my wife. She told me that one day I decided to stay Catholic and the next day I am an Episcopalian. My wife said I changed religions like I changed shirts. My wife is right in one respect. I kept changing my mind because if I stayed Catholic, I would never be a priest. If I would stay an Episcopalian, I might become an Episcopal priest. However, I disagree with both churches on some of their doctrines. In the Catholic church, even if a priest gives one absolution for his or her sins, that person still has to pay for those sins. He or she pays back partially by undergoing the penance that the priest gives. But the Catholic church has decided that the penance given by the priest does not completely make up for the sins committed. So, the penitent has to continue paying for those sins by prayer, attending Mass, almsgiving, visiting shrines, and doing good deeds. And, if the penitent still has not paid for his or her sins, the penitent goes to purgatory to be purged of sins before being allowed to enter Heaven. Yes, I do believe in purgatory; but I believe that purgatory is not a place of punishment; but a place for prayer and meditation—so that one can become close to Christ and be able to enter heaven. Purgatory is for Christians who believe in Christ but were never close to

Christ. People who are close to Christ will go directly to heaven after they die.

As for Catholics and Protestants they believe that Christ took upon Himself all the sins of the world—and so, instead of God punishing mankind, He punishes Christ. However, I could be wrong; but I believe that God could not punish Himself—that Jesus Christ is the Son of God and so the Son of God is God on earth; He does not have the purpose of punishing—His purpose is Love and that God is Love. Christ died on the Cross to show mankind that there was no question that He died in the Body of Jesus; but Jesus is also God and God cannot die—only the human body of Jesus died. By believing in the Resurrection of Jesus Christ, we as Christians would also be resurrected.

So, I am a little bit Catholic and a little bit Protestant and a little bit of what I believe that is neither Catholic nor Protestant. Many people say that this is not possible. The Catholic church believes that if one does not believe in all their doctrines, that that person is not Catholic. However, there are Catholics that some people call *cafeteria Catholics*—that they believe in what they themselves have convinced themselves to believe. Baptists believe that they have accepted Christ as their personal Lord and Savior. However, both the Catholics and Episcopalians believe that in baptism a seed has been planted in the baby's soul and, with the help of the baby's parents and godparents, that soul would grow and mature and will believe in Christ and the Holy Communion. The child of these churches would have to believe in Christ and the Holy Communion before they would be allowed to have their First Communion. So, this is the way that the child of these churches accept Christ as their personal Lord and Savior. It is not stated this way, but it is the same as accepting Christ in the Catholic and Episcopal and Baptist churches.

I believe in the sacraments of the Catholic and Episcopal churches because the Holy Spirit is present in all the sacraments. I may not believe in every Catholic, Episcopal, and Baptist doctrine, but I believe in Christ and in the sacraments of both the Catholic and Episcopal churches, and even the Baptist church baptism is a sacrament. In any case, I am a child of God and as a child I may be wrong in some of my beliefs; but, as a child, my Father will help me in my life. I am a child and so I believe that I am already in the Kingdom of Heaven—that I believe partly from my mind and partly from my heart. I do believe that the priest is an instrument of God when he gives absolution in confession or, as it is now called, reconciliation. But, I also believe as a Baptist that I can pray directly to God and that if I asked for forgiveness, God will forgive my sins and my sins will be forgotten. As a Baptist, I believe that Christ will guide me and help me so that I could not commit any terrible sin—that all my sins would be small sins.

The argument that I am having with my wife is whether I should be Catholic or not. I told my wife that if I could believe in the Immaculate Conception, I would stay a Catholic. The *Immaculate Conception* is Mary being born without original sin, so she is the Mother of God—the Mother of the Son of God. At first, I didn't even know what the Immaculate Conception was; I thought that this was just another description of Jesus Christ.

After I stopped talking with my wife, I went to the restroom. I was reading a book about Mary and the part I was reading was a description of the Immaculate Conception. Then, I saw a bright light on the floor of my bathroom. The light started rising and the light became a golden ball. Then, the golden ball broke apart and filled the bathroom with golden light. And then the light disappeared. I believe this vision was to teach me that the Immaculate Conception is real. This bathroom had no window and there was no way that any outside light could appear in that bathroom. So, I do believe in the Immaculate Conception—that this was God showing me that I should be a Catholic. I remembered that priest in the confessional at the Cursillo who said that God would show me the way that I should become in life. I believe that God was showing me that I should be a Catholic.

• CHAPTER 13 •

Kevin is transported back into the past and he sees the Crucifixion of Christ and a vision of a shining steel cross without Christ on it, signifying that Jesus Christ has been resurrected.

GOD

JASON, I KNOW THAT you are wondering what has happened to Kevin since he saw a vision of a golden ball that broke apart and filled Kevin's bathroom with golden light. Yes, Kevin had told his wife that if he could believe in the Immaculate Conception, he would only be Catholic. Well, Kevin did not stop going to the Episcopal church. He figured that it was possible that I wanted him to be an Episcopal priest. So, Kevin was still going to both the Catholic church and the Episcopal church. He figured that since he was already confirmed in the Episcopal church, and that he felt Me, the Holy Spirit, very deeply, maybe I wanted him to be an Episcopal priest. Kevin found out that the Bishop of Colorado in the Episcopal church in Denver had a school that taught young men about the Episcopal church and how to be an Episcopal priest in which young men could be ordained without going to a seminary. Well, Kevin applied to go to that school. The Bishop stated that it was too early for Kevin to attend his school since he was a recent convert—and that Kevin should get more involved in his local church and, later on, go to his school. Kevin had been attending the Catholic church for several years, and he believed that the Episcopal church was in reality a part of the Catholic church. So, he believed that he was not a recent convert. However, Kevin did get more involved in the Episcopal church: he became a delegate to help choose the auxiliary Bishop of Colorado, he joined the choir, and he went to the Men's Club of the church.

What happened is that one Sunday was stewardship Sunday. Laymen and the *vestrymen*, another way of saying they were the council men of the church, and the priest all gave speeches. What these men wanted was for the parishioners to give more money to their church. What they said was that if one does not tithe that person was not really a Christian—*tithing* is giving 10% of one's gross income to the church. And they said that a person is not a good Christian unless they gave more than the 10% of their income. Kevin was in shock. He did sign a pledge card stating that he could not give 10% of his income to the church, but that he would give what he could give. Kevin was giving $5.00 a week to the church. Well, the priest made a sarcastic remark that people were giving $5.00 a week in the time of the Depression. Well, Kevin was giving his $5.00 a week in envelopes that were put in the offering plate. So, the priest and the vestrymen and other men of the church knew that he was only giving $5.00 a week. Also, this local Episcopal church believed that if one was close to Christ one would be *prosperous*—meaning financially well-off. Kevin was having financial difficulties because he was an insurance agent who only got paid $97.50 a week to collect his policyholders' premiums. The rest of his paycheck came from the commissions that he sold, a part of which went into a sales account that was broken down into parts for his weekly paychecks. Kevin's debit or route were located into two small towns. Most of the policies that Kevin sold were small policies—these would not provide very much commissions. So, it was difficult for Kevin to give $5.00 a week to the Episcopal church, and he was giving $1.00 a week to the Catholic church.

Kevin had already contacted several Episcopal seminaries and they all required that the local vestrymen to recommend him to attend their seminary. It was then that Kevin believed that the vestrymen of his parish would not recommend him to go to the Bishop's school. They wouldn't give him a recommendation since he was not a good tither and that he was not prosperous. So, Kevin knew that he would never be an Episcopal priest because he could not attend an Episcopal seminary. Thus, Kevin decided to only attend the Catholic church.

After Kevin was only going to the Catholic church, he and his wife and his wife's sister and her husband decided to go on a vacation. They went to an Indian reservation which was close to Taos, New Mexico. They went to see that Miracle Wall in Holman, New Mexico. People were seeing a face of Christ on a wall on a church building that was only used for storage. Kevin and his wife and brother-in-law and sister-in-law wanted to see that face of Christ. When they drove into the parking lot of that building in Holman, they all saw Christ's face in a drawing of Christ—in dark ink—except for Kevin's brother-in-law. He didn't see anything. There were other drawings and Kevin had several visions. He was transported back into time in which he saw My Crucifixion. It is time for you to hear Kevin's thoughts.

KEVIN'S THOUGHTS

I and my wife and brother-in-law ad sister-in-law was on vacation. We went to Taos, New Mexico, and visited what is called Old Town; there, we went to see a nearby Indian reservation. On the way back home, we decided to visit Holman, New Mexico—a small town in the middle of the Sangre de Cristo Mountains. We wanted to go to Holman because we knew that people were seeing an image of Christ upon a wall of an old chapel that was no longer being used. As we drove up to that small church's parking area, we saw a large image of the face of Christ. The face of Christ was like a drawing of Christ in black. As we approached the wall, the large face of Christ no longer appeared on the wall. It was a bare wall. The wall was made of adobe and it had cracks and ripples in its structure. After we got closer to the wall, we saw a smaller image of Christ carrying His cross. Again, the image looked like an etching, a drawing in black. There were not many people there—maybe a dozen or so. Everybody was taking pictures. There was a little altar by the wall with candles and flowers placed there by the visitors. My brother-in-law and sister-in-law had gone back to the car. I must admit that I was looking for some trick or gimmickry on the wall. I was searching for a possible projector of some drawing that would only show from a certain perspective. I found nothing of the sort; the wall appeared to be normal, except for the drawings. But as one got closer to the wall, there were no drawings or etchings—only a bare wall.

Since my brother-in-law and sister-in-law were no longer at the wall, I and my wife took a walk around the church grounds and we saw a Catholic church. There were several people looking at the church. They were shouting and were very excited. We wanted to know what was going on. The people finally left and went back to their cars. I and my wife looked at the church and we did not see or hear anything. My wife then decided to go and find her sister and her sister's husband. I stayed, looking at the church. I was still wondering what had happened with those people as they were looking at the church. As I walked closer to the church, I saw images in between the windows of the church. These images were not black, but in brown. I saw an image of the Last Supper where Christ and the disciples were partaking of the First Holy Communion. By the next window, I saw an image of the empty tomb of Christ with a rock rolled away and an Egyptian chariot with one horse and no driver moving toward the empty tomb. By the next window, I saw an image of Christ standing with a shepherd's staff and a lamb in His arms. So, then I went to find my wife. I wanted to show her those images that I had just seen. I took her to the wall of the church. At first, I didn't see anything. Then, as I walked closer to the wall, I saw the images again. But my wife still couldn't see anything. So, this time I walked and touched the places where the images had appeared. But, as I walked to touch the wall, the images disappeared. The images only appeared from one position—so many feet away from the wall. Still my wife couldn't see the images. I took pictures of the wall, but those images did not show in the photographs.

It started drizzling and it was getting dark. My wife said that she was going to find her sister and brother-in-law as I was taking pictures. I was going to leave to join my wife when, all of a sudden, as I was looking at the wall, the wall of the church disappeared. I saw Jesus Christ upon the Cross. And it was dark. I saw Jesus from the side of the Cross so that Jesus was in profile. He was a large man. He was a strong and muscular man. It was so dark that His hair was in shadow; it seemed to be black hair. And upon His head there should have been a crown of thorns, but I could not see the crown of thorns; it was so dark that the crown of thorns looked like He had curly hair. And His head was bowed. I guess Jesus Christ was dying or that He had already died. This time, the Jesus that I saw was not a drawing or a painting or a shadow. I was actually there when Jesus was crucified. What I saw was real. It was as if I had been transported back in time. But it must not have been very long because my wife never came back for me. As I was seeing Jesus, all of a sudden a flash of lightning struck the streetlight that was just above the church. The light was not very far from me. The light went out very quickly, and then it came back on. This time, all I saw was a cross; but Jesus was not upon the cross any longer. It was a shining cross that seemed to be made of steel, but this time the cross was facing me; this Cross was not in profile. And then I had felt the rain hitting me. Apparently, as I stood there before this church wall, it was already raining. My wife had gone to the car where her sister and brother-in-law were. They had been there awhile and was wondering how come I did not come to the car. Still, I ran fast enough that I was not soaking wet. My wife wondered how I wasn't really wet—because it had been raining for quite some time. As we left, I told them what had happened. I was almost in shock; I had to reorient myself to realize that I was back in the car. I felt fresh and strong and alive. I felt good. I was not wet because I had been transported back in time.

• CHAPTER 14 •

Kevin sees the vision the Sacred Heart of Jesus.

GOD

JASON, I NEED TO tell you more about the life of Kevin after he saw Me die on the Cross. I should qualify that statement. I, as Jesus, did die in My human form; the human part of Me died. But, Jason, I, as Jesus, is still God and as God I could not die. So, he did not know what to do. All he could do was to continue living his normal life. He was an insurance agent, and he continued working at that job.

He did not tell anybody that he saw My Crucifixion, except for his wife, his wife's sister and her husband, and, eventually, his favorite priest in the Catholic church. He did not tell anybody else because he thought that people would think that he was crazy. In most people's minds, they could not believe that an ordinary man could be blessed by Myself to see My Crucifixion. So, Kevin had given up his dream of being an Episcopal priest and of being a Catholic priest; he was content to go to Mass that his favorite priest gave. His favorite priest really did give of himself; he was a charismatic priest who was a fantastic preacher and singer.

Even though Kevin and his wife went to Mass like any other normal Catholic, I chose Kevin to see another vision—what is called the *Sacred Heart of Jesus*. However, when Kevin did see this vision, he didn't know what he saw. He never paid attention to the statues and pictures of the Sacred Heart of Jesus. When Kevin was a Baptist, that church that he attended did not believe in the Sacred Heart of Jesus; they never said anything about this vision. And Kevin did attend the Disciples of Christ church when he went to college; and, again, there was no mention of this vision. So, Kevin didn't know what he saw. It took him a little while to figure out what he saw—because the Catholic parish that he went to changed. And because of this change, he was very depressed. The sisters that he worked with when he was in VISTA had left the parish and were assigned to another parish. The priest that Kevin became a friend to when he was in VISTA, the priest who came by to the senior citizen center that Kevin worked at, had given up the priesthood, gotten married, and moved to Michigan. The priest that married Kevin and his wife had left for another assignment. Kevin's favorite priest had also left for another assignment in another city. Kevin really missed the sisters and priests that he worked with and were his friends. Also, there was a young sister that Kevin became very close to and she, too, left and went to California. Yes, Kevin did still feel My Presence in the Mass. But still Kevin was depressed; he missed all his friends in the Catholic parish that he attended.

Kevin continued studying the Catholic church, and what this church believed as to his vision of the Sacred Heart of Jesus. Jason, I now will let you hear the thoughts of Kevin.

KEVIN'S THOUGHTS

I and my wife had gone to bed. As I was sleeping, I turned over and woke up seeing a flame above the head of my sleeping wife. Then, I noticed below the flame, but still above my wife's head, was a human heart. It was beating. With the beating of the heart was a stream of water, blood, and red roses; they were moving from the heart to a crucifix that was hung on the wall of our bedroom. The flow was moving very fast and flowed from the crucifix back to the heart that was above my wife's head. The heart wasn't a picture; it was a real heart. Red roses were interspersed throughout the blood and water.

When I first saw the flame and human heart, I did not know why I saw this and why that blood flow left that heart and went to the crucifix on the wall and then rushed back to the heart. I woke my wife up; but everything disappeared. My wife didn't see anything.

As time moved on, I wondered about what I saw and why I saw this vision. I noticed that there were statues and pictures of Christ showing a heart and flame in the middle of his chest. Not all statues and pictures showed that heart and flame; but some did. I found out that the heart and flame was called the Sacred Heart of Jesus. I never ever heard about the Sacred Heart of Jesus because I grew up a Baptist and the Baptists, and many other Christian denominations, did not believe in the Sacred Heart of Jesus. What I saw seemed very real; but, of course, on earth there would never be a human heart and flame that did not burn floating in midair. I knew this was a vision. I believe that God showed me this vision to show me that He is Love, and that He loved me. I remember what that priest told me in the confessional when I attended that Cursillo. He told me that God would show me whether I should be Protestant or Catholic. So, I believe that God was telling me that I should be Catholic because, in my own mind, I believed that only the Catholic church believed in the Sacred Heart of Jesus. Later on, I found out that there are other churches that believe in the Sacred Heart of Jesus; they are the Western Rite of Orthodoxy, the Anglican (Episcopal) church, and the Lutheran church. I found out that in those other churches only some of the members believe in the Sacred Heart of Jesus and many members don't.

I found out later that the Catholics pray the Rosary—that each bead of the Rosary represents a white rose and that the *Rosary* is a prayer to the Virgin Mary and to Jesus. The roses I saw in my vision appeared to be red—but as I think about this, blood would make a white rose look like a red rose. God was showing me that the Virgin Mary can be prayed for her intercession to God, especially to her Son, the Son of God. And only the Catholic church prays the Rosary. And the blood and water that flowed to the crucifix on the wall and back to the heart represents what happened when Christ was crucified. The Jews at that time did not want anyone on the Cross after sundown because after sundown the Passover celebration would start. So, a soldier stabbed Jesus in His side to make sure that Jesus was dead; and, when the sword entered Jesus, water and blood flowed from His wound. This water and blood were what flowed from the

Sacred of Heart of Jesus to the crucifix that hung on my wall. So, I believe that God was showing me that I should not only be Catholic, but that He loved me.

• CHAPTER 15 •

Kevin is saved by a little mongrel brown dog that fought off a big black dog that wanted to attack Kevin.

GOD

Jason, Kevin was not only having a hard time adjusting to life without the friendship of the sisters and priests that he worked with; but now Kevin has resigned from his job as an insurance agent. The economic recession had caused two factories to close in the two towns that Kevin worked as an insurance agent. Since most of his income had come from sales of insurance policies, when people lost their jobs they dropped their insurance, which made Kevin's sales account to fall very low. Kevin believed that since he was a college graduate, it would not take very long that he would have another job. But it was not that easy to find a job. Since he was a college graduate, he could not find an entry-level job. Those employers told Kevin that he was overqualified—that Kevin would find a better job and so Kevin would leave his employment with them. Those employers only wanted to hire high school graduates that would stay with them. The good jobs not only wanted a person to be a college graduate, they wanted to hire a person with experience. And Kevin did not have any experience, except working with people when he was in VISTA, when he was a senior citizen coordinator, and when he was an insurance agent. Kevin had taken several tests to be a caseworker; but he was told that they were looking for a person that was bilingual—to be able to speak Spanish. Well, there was an opening for a deputy sheriff in a mountain ski resort. He knew it would be a miracle if he would be hired since he did not know anything about firearms. But he was desperate; he had to find a job. Kevin had to go in person to fill out an application. So, Kevin did apply for that job as a deputy sheriff. But he was caught in a blizzard and could not drive home. There, a little brown mongrel dog saved Kevin's life. Jason, now listen to Kevin's thoughts.

KEVIN'S THOUGHTS

After my vision of the Sacred Heart of Jesus, God has not shown me any more visions. He has shown His love through unusual happenings. One day, I left my home early in the morning to apply for a job as a deputy sheriff in a mountain resort town many miles away from my home. It was in March and it was still cool, so I wore a light jacket. As I got closer to the mountains, it started to snow. The resort town was actually on top of a mountain. I drove to the top of that mountain and entered the town and submitted the application in person. As I left the courthouse, the snow on top of my car was six inches deep—and this was only for the half hour that I was in the courthouse. There were only two exits from that mountain resort and one of those exits was already closed due to heavy snow. The other exit that I first drove up the mountain was still open; it took me one hour to drive back down that mountain. When I got back down that mountain, it was raining. And it rained until I was only thirty miles from home. The snow and the wind became a blizzard. I could not see anything but snow—it was a whiteout. All I could see were the taillights of a car ahead of me. I followed those taillights and came to a town that was only ten miles from home. But the highway leaving that town was closed. I parked my car downtown and walked almost back out of town where my nephew lived. The lights of my nephew's home were all on throughout the house. I knocked on the door; there was no answer. I walked around the house and knocked on the back door; still there was no answer. I was getting very cold, and I did not even have a cap. Ice was forming in my hair. I had to get back to my car. I walked to my nephew's house because of the snow. There was a medium brown mongrel dog in the backyard. I did not see a doghouse or a bowl of food and water. I could see that the dog was also very cold. So, I told the dog to come with me and go back to my car—that I would turn my heater up and warm him. As I got closer to town, I noticed a bar that was still open. I left the dog outside, and asked the bartender when the highway would open up. He did not know; he said that the high school was where travelers could get out of the storm. I had parked my car further on down in the town and had walked past that bar when I was hoping to spend the night at my nephew's home. So, I and this dog started walking to my car. All of a sudden, I saw a big black dog—like a Great

Dane—charged at me. That dog by my side, charged that big black dog and drove the dog away. The dog by my side saved my life. It is as if that dog was my guardian angel. I and the dog went to my car, and I turned my heater on full blast. We went to the high school, and then I told the dog that it should go back home.Later on, my wife told me that she had spoken with my nephew who lived in that town where people were stranded due to a blizzard. The nephew told my wife that that dog was a mean dog—that no one could even get close enough to that dog to pet him. He said that he fed the dog once in a while. He said that the dog was a wild dog and was not his dog. Well, that dog did not even growl at me. That dog saved my life. God was with me and that dog.

• CHAPTER 16 •

Kevin struggles with his faith in finding a job and, not finding a job, he goes to graduate school.

GOD

JASON, I KNOW THAT you have just graduated from high school. You have not experienced exposure to a hard time finding a job, especially living under the hardship of being unemployed and having enough money to pay for the basic expenses for food, clothing, and shelter. Your parents are economically successful and have provided you not only the basic necessities of life, you had mostly anything you wanted. But Kevin was from a lower middle-class family. He did not have any luxury items. When he was in junior high, he had a TV guide route. In high school, he had a newspaper route, so he could buy clothes and some other items that his parents could not afford. You see, Jason, in some ways life is not fair. I designed the Earth so that mankind would have division of labor. After Adam and Eve ate of the tree of the knowledge of good and evil, they could no longer live in the Garden of Eden. Life outside was a cruel world compared to Eden. Mankind had to struggle in hunting animals for food and in the planting of crops. The weather brought storms and other natural catastrophes. Yes, I did help Adam and Eve and their children. But now, I would not be very close to them as I once was. I told Adam and Eve if they ate of the fruit of the tree of the knowledge of good and evil that they would die. I did not mean that they would die right away; however, spiritually they were already dead until I would bring back their inner spirit, which will be in the world outside of time and space.

Jason, the division of labor was necessary for living outside of the Garden of Eden, especially as civilizations grew with a population that kept growing as mankind reproduced themselves. What seems unfair about the division of labor is that men and women do not choose the family they were born into; they do not choose their level of intelligence, their race, even their nationality. And there has to be a difference in their intelligence so that this difference will determine what job or career children will take for most of their lives. The very intelligent people will be the leaders of society. They will run the government and make scientific discoveries and other matters for the general welfare of society. The people of lower intelligence will do the *manual labor*—jobs that require strength of the body to do physical labor. Yes, it is true that one can be lucky that even if he was born into an average family, he can be born with high intellectual capacity—so, that he or she can go to college and graduate school, medical school, or law school. If one doesn't have the intellectual capacity, that person could never be a doctor, lawyer, priest, minister, professor, or teacher. He would have to work hard and never make much money from his or her jobs. Yes, Jason, the leaders of society want to persuade people that they are all equal—thus, the phrase "created equal." This is not true and it could be considered the unfairness of life.

However, Jason, I pointed out what a lot of people would consider the unfairness of life. But there is more to life than having a good job, making a lot of money, or being seemingly more intelligent than the average person. I predestine some people so that with their effort to cooperate with Me, the Holy Spirit, their destination will be heaven. And other people can eventually be predestined to be called by Me so that they can enter the Kingdom of Heaven—which exists on earth in My Body, Christ—the Body of Christ in which the beginning of the Kingdom of Heaven is on earth and continues in heaven. These people who are saved by Myself, the Savior, are more fortunate than those of such high intellectual capacity, that they will believe that they do not need a Savior—that they can take care of themselves—so they do not believe in Me. Those people, in spite of their wealth and intelligence, can be very lonely. They can be spiritually dead and be worse off than the average man or woman who has been saved by Myself, by Christ.

Jason, I have predestined Kevin. However, there have been several tragedies in Kevin's life. You might ask, if I have saved Kevin, wouldn't his life be completely good and perfect with nothing bad happening to him? But, Jason, this is not how I have intended life to be on Earth. No matter how close a person is to Me, he will have moments of terror and disaster. This world is a testing ground to see who will still love Me, no matter what happens to their life. People who are saved will love Me no matter what happens in their life. The saved people are in this world but are not of the world—they are already entering into the Kingdom of Heaven while on earth, which will be fulfilled in heaven.

So, what happened to Kevin, after that dog saved his life? Kevin had resigned his job as an insurance agent. He resigned because his sales account became so low that he could not make a living selling insurance to low-income families who dropped their insurance when they lost their jobs in the recession that took place. Kevin did collect unemployment for a while. He did work as a sales associate for Montgomery Wards and Sears. He did teach school as a substitute teacher. But these were only part-time jobs. Kevin's wife was now going to a mental health center Mondays through Thursdays. He and his wife were living with his wife's mother. His wife's mental health center was in a town ten miles away from his mother's home. Kevin would drive his wife to that center and stay in that town until it was time for her to go home. Kevin stayed in that town where the mental health center was located because he was not very close to his mother-in-law. For lunch, Kevin would pick up his wife and go to McDonald's or have a picnic at the park. While his wife was at the mental health center, he stayed at the park. He would read and look at that beautiful park. On Fridays that his wife did not go to the center, he applied for work.

Since he did have experience working with people, he took the test to be a caseworker. He made a good grade, but he was not hired because they wanted somebody who was bilingual—to be able to speak

Spanish. Of course, Kevin was not bilingual; he was an Anglo from the Midwest. Finally, Kevin decided that if he was ever going to get a good job, he would have to go back to school. Since he already had a college degree, he had to go to graduate school. He applied and was accepted to study for an MSW degree in Social Work at a graduate school in St. Louis, Missouri—a city 900 miles from his wife's hometown.

At the mental health center, his wife's psychiatrist lowered the dosage of the medication that her wife was taking. But her wife had a relapse, so her medication was put back to what she was taking. Kevin then withdrew his application for graduate school. He wanted to take care of his wife. So, for one more year, he took his wife to the mental health center and he stayed at the park. His wife was doing really well. So, he sent an application to the same graduate school that he had applied for a year ago. He was told that he was already accepted; that his application was good for two years. So Kevin did go to graduate school; and his wife went to a mental health center in St. Louis. Jason, it is time for you to hear the thoughts of Kevin.

KEVIN'S THOUGHTS

When I lived in the West, after VISTA, I was a senior citizen coordinator. I did like this job, but it did not pay very well. My job as an insurance agent lasted thirteen years. Sometimes I did very well and many times I did not do very well in making a good living. I got paid to collect insurance premiums: I made commissions on the insurance policies that I sold. I worked in two towns with a combined population of 15,000 people. Most of my policyholders were of the lower economic class. So, I did not sell many big policies. So, I never made much money. As long as I could, I tried to manage my life accordingly. I was deeply in love with my wife. So, this helped me to not try to apply for other jobs—for a while. Then, two factories closed down in the towns that I worked in, so I quit my job as an insurance agent. When people lose their jobs, many people drop their insurance policies. So, I had a hard time making a living. I thought that since I was a college graduate, I could find a good job very quickly. This was not the case. I graduated from a liberal arts college—so, I knew a lot about many subjects—but I didn't have any job skills from any of the college subjects that I studied. I majored in History and Government, but I did not take any education courses that would have allowed me to teach those subjects as an elementary and junior high and senior high teacher. If I would go on to graduate school and receive a master's degree, I could be a college teacher. I did work at some part-time jobs, but none of those jobs were leading me to a career.

The career that I wanted wouldn't be just a job, but a dedication. I still feel the call to be a priest, which I could never be one being a married man. I love my wife and I've never regretted marrying her. I am upset that the Catholic church does not allow married men to become priests. In the Catholic church, the Eastern part of the church allow married men to become priests. The Catholic church now allows an Episcopal priest to become a Catholic priest providing that priest would go to a Catholic seminary and be ordained again. The new Catholic priest could be married and would be allowed to keep his wife and family. So, I thought there should be no reason why a married Catholic man could not be a priest. This seemed wrong to me.

Also, there are some Catholic priests that sexually abuse young people. And I ask myself "How can a priest do this?" A real priest would never abuse young people. I have an idea that might explain this, but this idea is not part of the Catholic doctrines. But it should be. I would have the sacrament of Holy Orders be like the sacrament of matrimony. When it is considered that one person in the marriage never understood the real meaning of the sacrament of marriage, the marriage can be annulled. And so, in the sacrament of Holy Orders, when a priest does not understand the real meaning of the sacrament of Holy Orders, his priesthood can be annulled. So, in effect, he was never a priest—so, I would be right in my thinking that a priest would never abuse young people.

If a married man in the Western part of the church could be allowed to be a priest, a married man could still take the vow of chastity. As long as a married man stays true to his spouse and never have any sexual relationships with other people, he would be chaste. So, considering my ideas, there could be married priesthood in both the Easter and Western parts of the Catholic church.

So, excusing my diversions of my explaining some of my ideas of what the Catholic church should be, I should continue stating what are some more reasons for deciding to go to graduate school. I did take tests to be a caseworker. And I applied to be interviewed in several counties in Colorado—where I and my wife lived. I made good marks and so was able to be interviewed, but I did not get hired. They were looking to hire someone who was bilingual—to be able to speak Spanish. I could not do this because I was an Anglo from the Midwest—from Illinois. Finally, I decided that the only way that I was going to get a good job is to have job skills. So, I decided to go to graduate school and earn a master's degree in Social Work. I went to school part-time and I worked part-time for Sears. I did this for two years and so I had one year of graduate study completed. I made good grades in all my classes. But for some reason, I could not pass the practicum. The *practicum* is supposed to teach one how to be a social worker—to apply what one learned in the classroom for working in the field. The grading for the practicum was only a pass or fail grade. The practicum, in my estimation, is not what it should be. My practicum instructors sat at their desks and gave out assignments of writing papers and filling out a notebook. There was no face-to-face contact with any patients. I wanted to be a medical social worker, so the practicums were in a hospital setting. My grades depended upon the subjective judgments of the practicum instructors, so I took two separate practicums—for I had to pass one practicum in order to graduate. The two practicum instructors that I had seemed to be biased women. In my judgment, they seemed to be man-haters. In any case, I did not pass my practicums, so I had to quit graduate school—or I should say that I flunked out of school. I couldn't afford to go to another graduate school; I had already borrowed too much money to go to graduate school in the first place. I was still working for Sears. I continued to take tests to be a caseworker, until finally I was hired. I worked as a caseworker and as a child support worker for a total of almost fifteen years. Then, I retired. I enjoyed my work for the

Department of Social Services in St. Louis, Missouri. Sometimes, I still wish that I would still be working instead of being retired.

Looking back on my graduate studies, in many ways I wish I had never gone to that graduate school. Not only was I disappointed in my practicums, I made a serious mistake. I and a Catholic sister took a practicum together—and I fell in love with her. I liked being with her; I liked talking with her. However, I still loved my wife. I thought "How is it possible to love two women at the same time?" Yes, I knew that some people step out on their wives and husbands, but most do it when they no longer love their spouses or they just want a sexual fling. Well, I never made a pass at that sister. I loved my wife so deeply that I would never break my marriage vows. But I became very close to that sister when we studied together and carpooled together. I never had a date with that Sister. I didn't intend to fall in love with her. But after I did fall in love with that Sister, I wanted to be with her—I thought we could remain friends—but not as girlfriend and boyfriend. I believed we were close to each other, and I believed that she was in love with me. But she knew that I loved my wife and would never divorce her. But I wanted to be close to her and be friends to each other. Even though I was in love with that sister, I wanted our relationship to be on a friendship basis. I would keep my vows of marriage; she would keep her vows as a sister. This was a mistake. A married man who loves his wife should never be close to another woman. All I can think of now is that my relationship with that sister should come to an end, even though I still love her. I even prayed to God that in some way we could still be friends. But our relationship stayed closed.

• CHAPTER 17 •

While thinking about that sister that Kevin loved long ago, he starts thinking about his past.

GOD

Jason, Kevin has been thinking about his past. Some of what has happened to Kevin may not seem to apply to you; however, there may be many things that will happen to you in which there may be more about Kevin's past that will be of help to you as you begin your adventure in life. So, Jason, now hear the thoughts of Kevin.

KEVIN'S THOUGHTS

Part of me still loves that Sister. However, it has been many years since we have seen each other. I might have changed enough that maybe I am a different person than when I was in graduate school. That sister may have changed, too, that we could be strangers to each other now. But, I do remember that Sister. And I was in love with her. And part of me still loves that sister as she was a long time ago.

My missing that Sister that I loved a long time ago has started me thinking what has happened in my life. In the beginning, I had my mom and dad for the first two years of my life. Then, when my dad finished his basic training, my mom and I took a train trip to El Paso, Texas—the base where my dad took his basic training after he got drafted during World War II. The very first sight that I can remember at two years old was what in my mind was a mountain of sand. I never saw such a landscape in Illinois where I was born. My mom raised me for two years by herself while my dad was stationed at Pearl Harbor. I am glad my dad was not at Pearl Harbor in 1941. He was there in 1944 to 1945.

My mom told me that occasionally I would wear one of my dad's army caps to sort of remember my dad. For those two years away from my dad, I clung to my mom and my grandmother, my dad's mom. My grandmother died when I was three years old; I do not remember her now. But how did I know that my grandmother came to me when I was with VISTA? I believe that internally my subconscious remembers the love that my grandmother gave me; so, I did know that it was her. I didn't see her or hear her, but I knew she was there. No one else has visited me after they have died. My mom told me that my grandmother used to go to the Disciples of Christ church, and that she was a strong believer in God. She even played the organ at that church. I believe that strong belief in God and the love that she had for me caused her to visit me and help me. I was lonely when I was in VISTA, until I met two people. Of course, the first person that I loved, and so I was no longer lonely, was the woman that I married. But, before I met my wife, it was Father Greg. He was the priest that would drop by the senior citizen center that I was operating. He would come almost everyday—Mondays through Fridays. He became my friend long before I knew anything about the Catholic church. He would drink a cup of coffee that I had made for the center. There were days that Father Greg was the only person that I saw at the center. So, I was lonely most of the time, until I started working with my senior citizens. Yes, I had a roommate that I hardly ever saw. Some nights he would not come home. The nights that he did come home, I was already in bed. I would leave the house to go to the center before he woke up.

My grandmother probably knew that I needed help to not feel so lonely. And, after my grandmother left my bedroom, from then on, I wasn't so lonely.

Knowing Father Greg gave me an awareness of the Catholic church before I ever had stood foot in a Catholic church. So, I thank God for having me to know Father Greg and for allowing me to feel the presence of my grandmother.

After my grandmother left my bedroom, I started to go to the Catholic church. I was helping the Catholic Sisters, driving them to conferences and setting up chairs and hymnals for at-home Masses. I started working with my senior citizens. I put on a variety show for the community, I put on a play about the Nativity, and I put on a religious pageant. I even believed that I was falling in love with one of the Sisters. She did leave the parish, not telling me goodbye. But, she did not know that I was falling in love with her.

I can thank God for knowing several priests and sisters, not in church but in their personal lives. In some ways, I even felt like I was a priest, since I was helping the sisters, helping the church, helping my senior citizens, and helping the community. I loved working with those priests and sisters, and I became very close to God in the Mass and in everyday life—so much that I thought about becoming a priest.

I can thank God for sending me to Rocky Ford, Colorado, my VISTA assignment, where I met the woman that I married. If I had never gone to Rocky Ford, I would never had met the woman who became my wife. And being married to Josie, my wife, was the best thing that I did in my life, besides being baptized and being confirmed.

I thank God that I was hired as a caseworker for the State of Missouri. I had taken the test to be a caseworker, but I was not hired. Later on, I found out what may be the reason that I wasn't hired. I found that out from a former supervisor of caseworkers in the county. He gave up being a supervisor in a welfare office to work as a child support worker in the city where I was working. He told me that he had quit working as a supervisor in that welfare office because of a lawsuit. Someone was suing the State of Missouri because in the county only Black people were being hired. And this was so because in all of the state offices in welfare and in child support were mostly young Black women. There were some white people, but very few. So, what happened was one Friday night, the office manager of that St. Louis county office in which the lawsuit was being carried out because of that office's policy of only hiring Black people, the office manager asked me if I still would like to be a caseworker. I told her yes. She told me to report to work on Monday—and this was without having to be interviewed. The State of Missouri was hiring everybody on their register for caseworkers. There were thirty of us on that register and I believe most of us were white. We all were hired without an interview. So, I thank God that I was hired that way—without having an interview. For whenever I was interviewed by Black supervisors, I was never hired.

Last, but not the least, I thank God for showing me supernatural visions and for Him showing me when He was on the Cross. In many ways, I am a little like a modern-day St. Thomas. I wanted to know God—not just to read about God. Just like St. Thomas, before he would believe that Jesus Christ was crucified, he said that he had to touch His wounds before he could believe that Jesus was resurrected. And Christ did show him his wounds and St. Thomas believed without touching Jesus Christ's wounds. And to be close to Christ, I had to see those visions and to see Jesus Christ on the Cross.

In some ways, I am like a modern-day Martin Luther, too. There were changes that he wanted to be done in the Catholic church. He stated those beliefs which were alien to some of the Catholic beliefs. He stuck to believing in those changes even when he was forced to leave the Catholic church. Marin Luther was a priest; and he did not want to leave the Catholic church; he only wanted to reform the Catholic church. Many of those changes that he wanted, were already made by the Catholic church. Why am I like Martin Luther? There are some changes that I would like to happen in the Catholic church and some changes that I would like for the whole Christian church. Yes, my changes probably will not take place, for I am part-Catholic and part-Episcopalian and part-Baptist and part of beliefs that are a little different and come from what I believe the Holy Spirit has shown me. In some cases, I may be somewhat wrong in my beliefs, but I feel that some of my beliefs come from the Holy Spirit.

• CHAPTER 18 •

Kevin's Life before Retirement

GOD

JASON, BEFORE YOU HEAR Kevin's thoughts, I need to tell you more about Kevin. As you know, Kevin had to quit graduate school. Actually, he did not quit; he failed to pass his practicums, and so he did not complete his graduate studies in working for a master's degree in Social Work. And it is very unusual that Kevin failed his practicums. Kevin made good grades in all his classes. Kevin was very upset. He had attended graduate school part-time for two years—so he had the equivalent of one year of graduate study. He had borrowed a lot of money to attend graduate school. Kevin could not afford to continue his graduate studies at another university—for he could not borrow any more money. And, now, he would have his student loans to pay back. He still had his part-time job at Sears and it paid very well for a part-time job because in addition to getting paid minimum wages, everything he sold paid him 3% commissions.

Kevin was also sad because he still missed that Sister he fell in love with. Yes, Kevin was still in love with his wife. While Kevin was still in school, he asked the director of the practicums if it's possible to love two women at the same time. He said that it is possible. Even though Kevin loved that sister, he had no intention to make love to that sister. He wanted friendship from that Sister and he wanted that Sister to be a friend to his wife. However, in his last year of graduate work, that sister already completed her studies and had went back to her convent. So, Kevin missed that sister in the last year of his studies, and now he was missing her even after he was no longer able to complete his studies.

Even though Kevin had a good part-time job at Sears, he did not want to spend the rest of his life working a part-time job. He did not know what to do. He could not afford to borrow any more money to go to another university to study for a master's degree. His past jobs were working with people and being a salesman. So, he decided to take the test to become a caseworker for the State of Missouri Division of Social Services. He made a good grade on that test. He had gone to several interviews, but he was not hired. He had thought that one reason why he was not hired was that he was white, and the interviewers were all black. Later on, he would find out that maybe that was the reason why he wasn't hired. Then, one Friday night an office manager called him and asked him if he still wanted to be a caseworker. Of course, Kevin said yes. He was told to report to work and, this time, without an interview. What Kevin found out from a fellow worker in the next cubicle was that there was a lawsuit against the State of Missouri because of one state office was only hiring Black people. That fellow worker was a supervisor in that state office and because of the lawsuit—and, in his estimation, the lawsuit was justified—he thought that it would be better to go to another office and become a child support technician, the same position that Kevin had. What the State of Missouri did was to hire people from the register who had made good grades without an interview. There were thirty of them that were hired without being interviewed. Kevin and those other people who were hired all took the training to help new workers to become caseworkers. All of them were white. And it is true that in all of the state offices in St. Louis, Missouri, most of the workers were young black women. There were some black men and a few white workers who were working in those state offices.

Kevin worked as a caseworker for one and a half years. He then applied to be a child support technician which, in reality, was a caseworker position with another title. Kevin worked at the Division of Child Support until he retired. Kevin, at first, was a regular child support worker; however, he became a customer service representative for several offices that he worked at. Before Kevin retired, he worked as a Parent's Fair Share technician. He worked for the State of Missouri for almost fifteen years.

Kevin did like working for the State of Missouri. And he was a happily married man. He retired at sixty-five years of age. He had promised his wife that if she would go with him to St. Louis so that he could go to graduate school and when he retired, he and his wife would move back to his wife's hometown. And that was what happened. Jason, it is now for you to hear the thoughts of Kevin at this time."

KEVIN'S THOUGHTS

After my wife was found to have a mental illness and when I applied to a graduate school which was one thousand miles away from my wife's hometown, my wife had a relapse from a reduction in her medication. However, my wife improved very quickly after received the full dosage of her medications. So, I withdrew my application for graduate school. I loved my wife very deeply, and I would not jeopardize her mental health in order for me to go to graduate school. In any case, I was afraid to go back to school. It had been around fifteen years since I had graduated from college. I didn't know if I could still study and make good grades. I would be going to graduate school in my forties, but I might be too old to become a college student again.

But, my wife did make quite an improvement in her mental health, so I decided to reapply to the same graduate school a year later. I was told that I didn't need to reapply; my application last year was good for two years.

My graduate school was located in St. Louis, Missouri. I went to work part-time at Sears in the daytime while my wife went to a mental health center Mondays through Thursdays. The center picked her up at the university and took her to the center; and, after her day was completed, they took her back home. In the evenings, I went to class. After one year of going to school part-time, in the summer I took a practicum. Well, I did not pass that practicum. It may have been this way because I fell in love with a Catholic Sister. She and I took the same practicum, and I drove us to a hospital for our practicum. I did not intend to fall in love with that Sister or any other woman; I loved my wife very much. As I drove that Sister to our practicum, I enjoyed talking with her; I liked being with her. And even though I fell in love with that Sister, I never made a pass at her. What I wanted was friendship from that sister; I even wanted that Sister to be friends with my wife. In any case, our relationship didn't work out. Since that Sister was going to classes full-time, she graduated and went back home to her convent. So, during the last year of my studies, I really missed her. I took another practicum the following summer, but I did not pass that practicum, too. It is very strange that I couldn't pass my practicum since I made good grades in all my classes.

I was very disappointed. I really wanted an MSW degree in Social Work; this did not work out. I had borrowed too much money to go to another graduate school. I was sad that I missed that sister; even though I was still in love with my wife. When I was taking my first practicum, I asked my director of practicums if it was possible to fall in love with two women at the same time. He said that it was possible. I believed that Sister was falling in love with me, too, but she was a Sister and, in her mind, it wasn't possible for her to give up her sisterhood. And I did not want her to stop being a Sister. I did learn that a married man should not be a close friend with another woman.

After I had failed my graduate studies, I was still working for Sears part-time. And for a part-time job, I did fairly well for I made 3% commissions on every thing I sold. Still it was only a part-time job. It wasn't possible for any of the new workers to have a full-time job. I did apply for manager training for Sears, but I never had any response for the resume that I had given the store manager; he was to give my application to the home office. I really didn't know if he had even sent my resume. When I was an insurance agent years ago, I applied for manager training at J. C. Penney; I was told that I was too old to take the training. I was in my late thirties. They said that after

I had finished their training, I would be too old to become a store manager before I would retire. So, this was probably why I was not given a chance to take manager training at Sears, when I was now in my forties.

The only other thing that I could think of was to again take a test to try to become a caseworker for the State of Missouri. I took the test and made a good grade. I went on several interviews, but I was not hired. Then, when I thought that I would not be hired as a caseworker, one Friday evening, an office manager of a county office in St. Louis County called me and asked me if I still wanted to be a caseworker. I told her yes, and she said to report to work on Monday—and this was without having to be interviewed. I did find out why I was hired without an interview later on, when I had transferred to be a child support worker. My fellow worker in the next cubicle told me what happened. He was a supervisor in the office where I worked, which was a welfare office. He transferred to child support and had the same position that I had. He said that he resigned as a supervisor because there was a lawsuit against the State of Missouri because in that welfare office, they were hiring only black people—mostly young black women. I did notice when I started working in that office that there were few white people working. Most the workers were black, and most of the supervisors were black. Also, when I took my training, all of us trainees were white. My fellow worker told me that the State of Missouri hired everyone on the registrar for the caseworker position who had made a good grade and were white—this was because of the lawsuit. All of us trainees from that registrar took our training together and we didn't have to be interviewed.

There were thirty of us trainees and, when we were assigned to work, we worked at several offices in St. Louis.

I enjoyed my work at the Division of Social Services. I worked there for almost fifteen years. I retired at sixty-five years of age. I had promised my wife that if she would go with me to St. Louis to go to graduate school, and possibly to work in St. Louis after graduating, when I retired, we would move back to Rocky Ford, Colorado—my wife's hometown. So, after I retired, we did move back to my wife's hometown.

I want to say, thank you, God, for helping me to get hired as a caseworker. I had gone on several interviews and was never hired. To be hired without having to take an interview is very rare. God did help me.

• CHAPTER 19 •

Kevin's Life after His Wife Died

GOD

JASON, MAYBE I SHOULD not talk to you about the situation that Kevin is in, but I feel that you should know what to expect in this lifetime. I know that in some ways you do know; but, it is something most people do not want to think about, especially at your age. You are only eighteen years old, but you are old enough to talk briefly about Kevin's situation. Kevin's wife died. His wife had many illnesses, and Kevin was his wife's caregiver. However, Kevin did not expect that his wife would die. He had got up early and made coffee. He watched TV for a while. Then, he went to his bedroom to wake up his wife to have her come and eat breakfast. But Kevin could not wake her; she had died in her sleep.

Kevin, all people die; some die when they are young, some die when they are older. But this is the way that I have designed the world. Everyone dies at some point in time. Even the animals die.

Kevin took the death of his wife very hard. When the police came—the officer had been married to his niece, so Kevin was close to that police officer—Kevin hugged him and cried. He did not know what to do. He did not feel like doing anything. His nieces told him to come and stay with them, but Kevin said no. The next day, Kevin and his two nieces went to the Catholic church to plan the Funeral Mass. Then, Kevin and his two nieces went to pick out his wife's casket and the design for her tombstone. Kevin was sort of in limbo. He only thought about leaving and to live in his sister's town that was a thousand miles away. Kevin had a hard time living in the apartment that he and his wife had lived in. He had a hard time sleeping in the same bed that his wife died in. He had a hard time shopping and seeing the restaurants that he and his wife had gone out to eat. So, Kevin did decide to move and live in the same town that his sister lived in. He was not going to take his furniture; he even wasn't going to take very many books. He had a yard sale and he donated some of his wife's things to a thrift shop. He did keep some of his wife's things: some of her angels that she had collected, some of her books, some of her towels and scarves that she had embroidered. What he would take would have to fit into his car. He would stay with his sister and brother-in-law until he could move into a senior citizen complex. He stayed with his sister and brother-in-law for about a month and a half.

But, now Kevin was alone. He was a widower. He had no children—only his sister and brother-in-law. He still kept in touch with his nieces and nephews that still lived in his wife's hometown. He also had a sister-in-law that was also his niece who lived in Texas. But, now there was no face-to-face communication—only by phone. Kevin did make some new friends and one woman that he loved. That woman friend helped him to not be so lonely; they watched TV and played cards. But, Kevin is now seventy-eight years old; he thought he was too old to marry again.

Kevin does eat with some friends in the community room; the meals were delivered by Community Action. He does go to Mass. He does experience My Presence in the Mass. And when one experiences My Presence in the Mass, it is a beautiful and wonderful experience. Kevin still misses his wife, but he feels that he will see her again in heaven. So, Jason, it is now time for you to hear Kevin's thoughts.

KEVIN'S THOUGHTS

I retired from my job as a child support worker. I promised my wife that if she had gone with me to a city a thousand miles away from her hometown so I could go to graduate school, when I retire from whatever job I would have after graduate school, I and her would move back to her hometown. And this is what we did. My wife's hometown was not the same as before when we first lived there. It has been seventeen years. My wife's brothers and one sister had died. I was very close to my wife's brothers. We could talk to each other just about everything in our lives. So when I did live in my wife's hometown before I went to graduate school, I really did enjoy visiting and talking with my brothers-in-law and one sister of my wife. She had died before I and my wife moved back to my wife's hometown. My wife still had one sister that was still alive. I loved that sister-in-law like a real sister, but I never talked with her like I did with her brothers. My wife had a niece that was raised by her mother as a daughter—so my wife has a sister. This person is still alive, and I love her like a sister, too.

When I first lived in my wife's hometown as a VISTA volunteer and a senior citizen coordinator, I had several senior citizens that were my friends. Those senior citizens have died. I was a friend to several priests and Catholic sisters, and they have all gone to work at other parishes in other states. So all my friends had either died or had moved away. My wife's nieces and nephews and that one sister that is still alive are still living in that hometown, except for one sister who lives in Texas. They still call me uncle and I do visit them. But it is not the same when I was close to those nieces and nephews' parents. So, the only person that I could talk with about everything was my wife. We were close to each other and loved each other very much. I was close to my sister and brother-in-law and my mother who lived in the Midwest where I lived for seventeen years. But since they lived a thousand miles away, I kept close to them by talking with them on the phone. Still it isn't the same as being with them in a face-to-face relationship. So, the only person that I had a personal relationship with was my wife.

My mother died in that town a thousand miles away. For a while, I talked with her on the phone and she could talk with me. And then, she had a stroke and she could no longer talk; but I still talked with her anyway until she died. I and my wife went to her funeral. My dad had died seven years before my mother did. So, now I no longer had my parents alive. With my parents being alive, where they lived was my home. I had a place to go to that was my home no matter where I lived on planet Earth. Yes, I still had my sister and brother-in-law, but they had their own homes and lives to live in which I'm in a way an outsider. I love them very much, but one only has one's parents in which one would never be an outsider in their lives.

I and my wife, after my mom's funeral, went back to where we lived in my retirement. And for two more years, we lived out our lives with love—even when my wife started to get sick. She had many illnesses; I was her caregiver, and in some ways we were even closer to each other as I took care of my wife. My wife eventually had her right leg amputated above her knee. She did have an artificial leg, but she couldn't walk very far; she would get very tired. So, for the next five years she was in a wheelchair. Then, she died. And it seemed that my life was over. I loved my wife very much and we had been married for almost forty-five years. Now she was gone. I could not take it living in the same apartment that I and my wife lived in. Even seeing the restaurants and stores that we went to reminded me of my wife so much, that I could no longer live in my wife's hometown. I was very lonely. So, I decided to move back to the Midwest and live in the same town where my sister and brother-in-law lived. However, without my wife, I am still lonely. I do have a personal relationship with my sister and my brother-in-law. I speak to my sister on the phone every day; I usually see my sister and brother-in-law once a week in my sister's home. I live in a senior citizen complex, and I have several friends that I share a meal with for lunch five days a week. I have a woman friend that I love. That woman helps me to not be so lonely. We go out to eat, we watch movies on TV, and we play cards. But since I am seventy-eight years old, I am probably too old to be married again. But, I do love her and we see each other quite often. When I am not with my woman friend, I am still lonely. In some ways I shouldn't be lonely. I am close to God and I do feel the Holy Spirit during Mass. I would hope some day to be filled with His Love, His Joy, His Peace—but this will be when I hope to be with Him in heaven. I do thank God that I am able to be close to Him and to love Him. One day, I will again be close to my wife in heaven.

• CHAPTER 20 •

God's Last Comments to Jason

GOD

JASON, IT IS ABOUT time for you to wake up. But, before you do this, I have to tell you a little more about Kevin. Jason, because I have shown you Kevin's life, you should learn from the experiences of your dream and start to live your life spontaneously. I will help you, but I will be in many ways hidden from your immediate knowledge that I am helping you. You must become a person who has to make your own decisions about your future—such as your choice of career, your choice of religious faith, your choice of what college or vocational school to attend to follow your educational goals, your mate to share your life with and to love for the rest of your life. Yes, I did help Kevin by showing him visions. And why did I do this? Kevin is like one of My apostles, St. Thomas. Thomas had to see the wounds that I have from being tortured and crucified. He had to see with his own eyes what the other disciples were telling him—for when I first appeared to the disciples, he was not there. When I appeared to the disciples again, Thomas was there. I showed him My wounds, but

Thomas didn't have to touch My wounds when he declared My Lord and My God.

Like Thomas, Kevin was always skeptical about many things. Take the Bible. This book has been passed down from generation to generation. Most people learn their faith by being taught by the Bible, by ministers and priests, by Sunday school teachers and catechists. Most people believe what they are told. But Kevin did not just believe. He wanted to know Me, and to not just read about Me. And My visions have helped him to know Me and My Mother, Mary. Yes, no man or woman will ever know Me completely—not even in heaven—for I am God. Jason, most men and women, including yourself, won't have the visions that I gave Kevin. I did give you supernatural experiences in your dream. But, when you wake up, I do not talk to people like I am speaking with you in this dream. Most people will not see Me die on a Cross. Most people will not be like St. Thomas and Kevin. Yes, I did let Kevin see Me on the Cross. Why did I do this to Kevin? I wanted him to know that I had to die on the Cross to show people that I died. In the time that I, as Jesus, died on the Cross, people would see Me die on that Cross. And the future generations of mankind will read about my Crucifixion, and the priests and ministers will talk about My Crucifixion. But, Jason, I surrendered Myself to evil and had the human part of My body die. But, I didn't come to Earth to be punished for mankind's sins. I came to die because mankind does sin—to show them that mankind alone without Me, will die just as My human part died on that Cross. Jason, My body is not only man, but God. Not even evil can kill God. But,

Jason, when I transported Kevin back to his own time, I showed him another Cross that was all light; the cross appeared to be steel. But I was not on that Cross. This was to show Kevin that I was resurrected. And mankind, if they believe that I was resurrected, will be resurrected after they die as long as they are baptized by water and by Myself as the Holy Spirit. They will be part of the Kingdom of Heaven here on earth before they die; they will be my sons and daughters on earth and in heaven.

Besides Kevin being like a modern-day St. Thomas, he is somewhat like Martin Luther, too. Kevin was part-Baptist, part-Disciples of Christ; part-Christian Scientist, part-Lutheran, part-Presbyterian, part-Pentecostal, and part-Catholic. The first church that Kevin went to was a Presbyterian church. That was the church where Kevin saw that angel fly out of the steeple. Kevin was ten years old. The second church that effected Kevin was the Lutheran church. That was the church that gave sunrise services on Easter when his parents went to the local drive-in theater for these. The Lutheran church gave the services. The next church that Kevin went to was the Baptist church. The next church was the Disciples of Christ church. Kevin went to Eureka College in Eureka, Illinois, and that church sponsored that college, so Kevin went to that church for the four years that he went to college. The next church that Kevin was exposed to was the Christian Scientist church. When Kevin was going to the University of Missouri to study Theater Arts, his roommate was a Christian Scientist, a devoted Christian Scientist. When Kevin had to drop out of that university, he was very depressed—for in college he was a college scholar and graduated summa cum laude. He had to drop out of that university before he flunked out. His roommate knew he was very depressed. He sent him a copy of the Christian Scientist manual written by Mary Baker Eddy. And that book was very beautifully written. Kevin did read that book. And the first church that Kevin went to when he was in Rocky Ford, Colorado—Kevin's assignment—was a Christian Scientist church. There was no music. There was one reader who read from the Bible and one reader who read from Mary Baker Eddy's book. But, there were only a few people in attendance, and all the people seemed to have colds and did a lot of coughing. Kevin, in his mind, knew that even though Mary Baker Eddy did write a beautiful book, it wasn't part of the reality of the Kingdom of God. So he never went back to that church.

The next church that Kevin went to was the Roman Catholic church. He was a VISTA volunteer who worked with mostly Spanish and Mexican senior citizens. They were all born Americans, but most of them went to the Catholic church. Kevin went to that church to understand the culture of his senior citizens. And, as you know, Jason, found out that the Holy Eucharist was real. The sisters asked him if he could help them, since he was a VISTA volunteer. They wanted him to drive them to conferences and to help move chairs and place hymnals on chairs at home Masses. And Kevin did help out. He eventually felt that I was calling him to become a priest. One of the sisters gave him some books to read about the Catholic church. As you know, Jason, that Kevin fell in love with one of his senior citizens' daughters. He married her and so could no longer become a priest. Kevin always went to Mass, even though he was married. He still felt like I was calling him to be a priest. He wondered if there was a church that was very similar to the Catholic church—for Kevin did believe in all the seven sacraments of the Catholic church. He found out that the Episcopal church was quite Catholic. So, he did go to the church on Sunday mornings and to the Catholic church on Saturday nights. Jason, you do know what happened to Kevin; he no longer goes to the Episcopal church. The next church is what Kevin calls Pentecostal; but, in the Catholic church, it is called *charismatic*—and Kevin's favorite priest was a charismatic priest. Now, Kevin did go to the Full Gospel church in Lincoln, Illinois, where his sister lived. He was still going to the Catholic church; however, there was a famous Pentecostal singer and minister who was going to have a service at that Full Gospel church. That minister had people go forward and he placed his hands on the people and baptized them with the Holy Spirit. So, Kevin did go and was baptized by the Holy Spirit. Kevin only went to that church to see that minister. He had no idea that he would be baptized with the Holy Spirit. He still goes to the Catholic church and he remembers that favorite priest who was charismatic. He only goes to the Catholic church and he believes in all of its seven sacraments. But, he did feel the Holy Spirit in that Full Gospel church. He remembers that he has been baptized twice—once in the Baptist church and one in the Catholic church. And he remembers when he was confirmed in the Episcopal church in which he was sealed by the Holy Spirit. So, Kevin is a mongrel Christian. He calls himself Catholic since believes in all the sacraments of the Catholic church, and he goes to Mass every Saturday night.

Why is Kevin like a modern-day Martin Luther? It is because he has experienced Myself, the Holy Spirit, in many different churches. There are some beliefs of the churches that Kevin has attended that he does not believe. The Catholic church believes that even if a person has gone to confession and their sins have been absolved, that person still has to pay for these sins. The priest gives a penance to the penitent as part of his punishment for sinning. But, they believe that this penance is not enough punishment for their forgiven sins. They have to continue to pay for those forgiven sins by going to Mass, by prayer, by giving alms to the church, by visiting one of the church's shrines. Then, if a person has not sufficiently paid for his or her sins on earth, then he or she goes to purgatory to continue to be purged of these sins. He believes a priest has the ability to have the Holy Spirit to forgive people's sins. But, as a Baptist, he still believes that one can pray directly to God and He can forgive one's sins. And once those sins are forgiven, they are forgotten. There is no required punishment. Kevin still believes that he has accepted Me as his personal Lord and Savior, and he still prays to Me that his sins will be forgiven.

Kevin believes in purgatory. But, he believes that purgatory is not a place of punishment. He believes that purgatory is where people who believe in Myself, the Christ, but have not been very close to Myself, the Christ, the Holy Spirit, and God the Father. So, purgatory is a beautiful place. People go there to become closer to Christ. It is a place of meditation and beauty. And once they become close to Christ, they will go to heaven.

As for all the Christians churches, including the Catholic church, the Bible states that hell is where people are burned forever. Kevin does not believe that; he believes that hell is a beautiful place and that no one is burned. Hell is for evil people and what makes hell evil is not real fire, but the fire of the anger of the minds where evil people become hell to one another.

Kevin believes that his wife, Josie, is in heaven. And he believes that since he was married to Josie for almost forty-five years and that he and his wife were deeply in love with each other, even if the Bible states that there is no marriage in heaven, Kevin still believes that he and Josie will still be married to each other and that they will be able to still live with each other.

As you know, Jason, Kevin believes that there should be a married priesthood for the whole Catholic church. Martin Luther did not want to leave the Catholic church, he only wanted to reform the church. Kevin wants to reform the church, too, but he knows that he is not a Martin Luther. Still, he hopes to change the church, if not in his lifetime, maybe in the future generations.

So, Jason, be your own person. The church where you feel the Holy Spirit the most is the church that you should attend—even if it is not the Catholic church.

Jason, learn to accept the Love of God, and learn to love God. Pray to God and learn how to be guided by God and to follow Him as your Lord and Savior.

Index of Visions and Supernatural Manifestations

Kevin sees an angel—Chapter 2

Kevin is baptized in the Baptist church—Chapter 3

Kevin experiences the Holy Spirit observing Holy Communion—Chapter 7

Kevin feels the presence of his deceased grandmother—Chapter 7

Kevin gets married and feels the Holy Spirit—Chapter 8

Kevin gets rebaptized in the Catholic church and feels the Holy Spirit—Chapter 9

Kevin is confirmed in the Episcopal church and feels the Holy Spirit—Chapter 10

Kevin feels the Holy Spirit partaking in the Cursillo—Chapter 11

Kevin sees a bright light on his bathroom floor. The light rises and forms a golden ball. The ball continues to rise and breaks apart filling the bathroom with golden light. This happens when Kevin was reading about Mary—the Immaculate Conception—Chapter 12

Kevin is transported back into the past and sees the Crucifixion of Jesus Christ—Chapter 13

Kevin sees a vision of a steel cross that is all in light. Jesus Christ is not on that cross, signifying that Jesus Christ was resurrected—Chapter 13

Kevin sees drawings on a chapel wall and on the wall of a Catholic church. The drawings were between the windows of that church—Chapter 13

Kevin sees the vision of the Sacred Heart of Jesus—Chapter 14

Kevin is attacked by a large black dog. A mongrel minimum sized dog attacks the large black dog. The dog saves Kevin's life. His nephew stated that the mongrel dog was a mean dog and no one could even touch that dog—Chapter 15

Kevin is hired as a caseworker without being interviewed—Chapters 17 and 18

Author's Note

MY BOOK IS PARTIALLY fiction and partially non-fiction. The non-fiction part of my book is what happens to Kevin. Kevin in real life is me. What happens to Kevin is what really happened to me. Why didn't I write an autobiography? It's because I want my readers to identify themselves with Kevin. Kevin is a fictional character and people can identify themselves more easily with him than they can identify themselves with a real person, like me. Also, for the readers to identify themselves with me can be almost impossible for many people. What has happened to me is extraordinary—so much so that people might not believe me; or they would think that I made up my story; or they might think that I am crazy. Also, I do not have a degree in religion or theology. However, I am close to God; His Holy Spirit has helped me to write this book. But if the book is strictly fictional, people might believe Kevin. The book is fictional because there is no Kevin; there is no Jason; there is no God who communicates to Jason. Yes, there is a real God in real life, but God usually does not talk to a person whether in real life or in a dream—which was the way God in the book talks to Jason.

I would hope my book might cause some people to believe in God. I would hope some people might want to go to church to learn more about God and to worship God. I would hope that some people would just go to the Catholic church and observe the Mass. They might feel the Holy Spirit like I do when I go to Mass. I would hope some people would go to church and be a believer in that church. The church that a person should belong to is the church in which that person feels the Holy Spirit very deeply—to feel the Holy Spirit in their mind and in their heart. Yes, that church can be Catholic, and it can be a Protestant church.

I hope in some way that I can reform the Catholic church and the Protestant church. I call myself Catholic; however, I have some Baptist beliefs that I had when I was twelve years old. At that age, I had to believe that Jesus Christ exists; and I had to accept that Jesus Christ is my personal Lord and Savior. I had to believe this in order to be baptized in the Baptist church. I still believe that I have accepted Jesus Christ as my personal Lord and Savior. Even if I do believe in the Sacrament of Reconciliation (also called Confession—which I do believe), as a Baptist I was taught to pray to God directly and to ask for forgiveness of my sins; and, if the sins are forgiven, they are forgotten. God does not remember forgiven sins; it is as if that person had never committed the forgiven sins. The Catholic church believes that a person must pay for forgiven sins. They believe that the penance that the priest gives the penitent does not sufficiently make up for the sins that the person has confessed. They believe that to make up for their forgiven sins they can do so by going to Mass and receive Holy Communion; that one would pray to God; that one would give alms to the church; or to visit a shrine. The Catholic church believes that if a person has not paid enough for their forgiven sins on Earth, then that person after he or she dies would go to purgatory to be purged—punished for their sins. Then, after they are purged or punished, that person would go to heaven. Yes, I do believe in purgatory, but it is a beautiful place in which a person can pray to God and to meditate. It is not a place of punishment. Purgatory is a place of love and meditation. I believe purgatory is where a Christian goes if one believes in Christ, but is not close to Christ. He goes to purgatory to be close to Christ so that if he or she does become close to Christ, then, they would go to heaven. Yes, I do believe in hell; but I believe that it is a beautiful place, too. God never creates ugliness and devastation. Hell is where the evil people go after they die. The people there are not burned by fire; hell is being with other evil people.

Also, I believe that the Western part of the Catholic church allows married men to become priests.

How would I reform both the Catholic church and the Protestant church? Both churches believe that God the Father sent His Son to be punished for mankind's sins. I believe that the Son of God is a manifestation of God; He is God. God would not go to Earth to punish Himself. I believe that God died on the Cross to show people that He really appeared to die. And in His human form, His body did die. Jesus appeared to surrender to Evil. But it is only an appearance. Yes, Jesus' human body did die; but God cannot be killed. Yes, Jesus Christ loved us and to show His love, besides His suffering and human death, He showed the world that He was resurrected. And if we believe that Jesus Christ was resurrected, then after our death, we will be resurrected. I believe that God is the ultimate of Love and Goodness; He does not harm anyone; all He does is out of Love.

I am little bit Catholic, a little bit Protestant, a little bit of my own beliefs. I thank God for showing me visions and for transporting me back in time to see His Crucifixion. So, I am little bit like St. Thomas. He had to see the wounds of Jesus before he would believe that Jesus was resurrected. So, in a lot of ways, I had to not just read about God, I had to be shown that God is real—even when I was ten years old, I asked to see an angel.

I am a little bit like a modern-day Martin Luther. He wanted to reform the Catholic church; he did not want to leave the Catholic church. So, I am a little bit like Martin Luther, I want to change the Catholic church and the Protestant church. Yes, he was a priest; he was forced out of the Catholic church. But some of his reforms have been changed in the way he wanted the Catholic church reformed. Maybe my reforms will not take place; I have no authority like Martin Luther. I am not a priest, I do not have the knowledge that he had. I do not have the holiness of Martin Luther. I believe that the Catholic church should make him a saint. But wanting reforms makes me a little bit like Martin Luther. And I do believe that the Holy Spirit has guided me in my beliefs.

I want to thank my readers for having the patience to read my book. I am not saying I am completely right in all my beliefs, but I do believe that I am right in many of my beliefs. I hope the Holy Spirit will guide you in your faith journey.

With the Love of Christ,

Jerry Kneeland

About the Author

I GRADUATED FROM EUREKA College with a B. A. Degree in History and Government.

I graduated from the University of Colorado with a Vista Training Certificate having the equivalent of 8 graduate semester hours in Social Work.

I was a Vista Volunteer for one year.

I have one year of graduate work in Social Work from St. Louis University.

I was married to my wife Josie for 44 years and 10 months. My marriage was one of my best accomplishments. Marriage is a Sacrament of the Catholic Church . I was "Christ" to my wife and she was "Christ" to me.

I am a retired life insurance agent and a Social Service worker for the State of Missouri.

My wife died in 2015. I started writing this book after my wife died. Writing this book has helped me to live without Josie. It has helped me to relive my spiritual experiences and to be closer to God.

www.ingramcontent.com/pod-product-compliance
Lightning Source LLC
Chambersburg PA
CBHW071518040426
42444CB00008B/1703